Fifth Edition

HULL
The Heavenly Pottery

By

Joan Gray Hull

An Alphabetical, Numerical, Pictorial, Pocket Size
Price Guide for Hull Pottery Lovers

Copyright 1997

Joan Gray Hull
1376 Nevada SW
Huron, SD 57350
Telephone: 605-352-1685

ISBN
0-9627078-5-6

Darlene Kutzler, Photographer

Printed by
Creative Printing
210 Third St. SW
Huron, SD 57350

©1997

CONTENTS

CONTENTS

ACKNOWLEDGEMENTS

It took years of encouragement from the many Hull collectors and dealers across the country before I actually began the undertaking of "HULL THE HEAVENLY POTTERY".

I am amazed at the number of letters and calls I have received from all over the United States from people who tell me how much they love the alphabetical, numerical pocket sized price guide of each edition of "HULL THE HEAVENLY POTTERY". I am so happy to know that the book is as much desired by you as I thought it would be. I appreciate each letter or call that you have taken the time to send me.

I began collecting after my husband's death when a friend, Joy Johnson, bought a piece of Hull at a rummage sale and gave it to me saying, "With a name like Hull, you should be collecting it." The suggestion took and I began searching antique shops and flea markets of the first time in my life. (I highly recommend new hobbies for grief therapy.) Collecting has changed my life. After 20 years, I now own approximately 2000 pieces of this lovely pottery.

My deep appreciation goes to my photographer, Darlene Kutzler, for her hard work. Without Dee Konyha, the First Edition could never have been printed. John Burks sent a number of updated pictures for the Second Edition. The Third Edition was greatly enhanced by pictures from the late Gayle McGooden's extensive collection. Lon & JoAnn Higginbotham, Joe & Betty Yonis, and Mary Ann Boddy added a great deal to the fourth edition.

HULL THE HEAVENLY POTTERY is designed to be a price guide only. Avid Hull Collectors should have Robert's "ULTIMATE ENCYCLOPEDIA OF HULL POTTERY" for a complete History of the company including trademarks and labels. Hull collectors are also urged to add Barbara Burke's "A GUIDE TO THE HULL POTTERY COMPANY DINNERWARE LINES" to their book collection.

Throughout the year I receive many pictures, suggestions and information to be used in my books. How I wish I could name and acknowledge each of you, but that is impossible. Please know how much I appreciate each one of you who helped in any way to enhance this fifth edition of "HULL THE HEAVENLY POTTERY".

Hull's number system is extensive and very confusing to the new collector. Most designs bear a different type of trademark. Some Stoneware pottery is marked with a number and an ⊕ or a ⬦. The popular matte finished Hull pieces are also marked in a number of ways: some are in raised letters, some incised, some blocked, and some are in script writing. Kitchenware items' trademarks usually include the words Oven Proof. Molds manufactured after 1950 are often in script writing. The most modern florist planter type molds often show Hull written with the small "h".

Letters, as well as numbers, are used on some designs to help the collector identify the pattern.

The lucky collector may find pieces of Hull pottery with the original label still on the vase. Most of the labels are the triangle shaped label in black with the words Hull Pottery in silver or gold, or the round label bearing a picture of a Potter-at-Wheel and the words Hull Pottery Crooksville, Ohio printed in silver or gold. Other labels with other markings and/or colors can be found. Labels should add $5 to $10 value to each vase depending on the condition of the label.

PRICING

Collectors and dealers from New York to Florida, from California to Idaho, Michigan, Nebraska, and many points in between have sent me their price lists to be averaged. Prices will be affected by the condition of the vase, labels, gold trim, unusual finishes, color, and other variables.

Since the dinnerware lines are coming more increasingly collectible, I am enclosing as many pages as possible in this Fifth Edition.

Since the First Edition of HULL THE HEAVENLY POTTERY, I feel some prices of Hull have become almost outrageous. Prices in Bowknot, Little Red Riding Hood, and the Wildflower numbered series have climbed 25% to over 100% of the published prices. As a collector, I don't see how these prices can continue to rise at such rates or most of us will not be able to afford to add to our lovely collections.

Other items that seem to have risen drastically are the larger vases, pitchers, and baskets. I understand these price increases in the rarer hard to find pieces.

I have received many requests to put prices on the items marked rare. I'm attempting to price some of them in this edition. However, I feel I have no right to price "one-of-a-kind" items that I don't own or that owners have no intension of selling. The price should be their choice, not mine.

The deeper we are into collecting and research of Hull, the more we understand which pieces are the rarest and command the higher prices. As always, some prices will seem too high in one area and too low in another. Prices are to be used only as a guide. The owner does not have to sell a piece of pottery for any less than he wishes. By the same token, the buyer does not have to buy any item that he considers over priced.

Hull pottery designer, Louise Bauer, pictured in her charming home, is holding a Parchment & Pine basket she designed. Louise began contracting her artwork to the Hull Pottery Company in 1949 and continued designing until the plant closed in 1986. She designed Bow Know, Woodland, Little Red Riding Hood, Serenade, Ebb Tide, Butterfly, Blossom Flite, Tokay, Tropicana, and hundreds of other novelty items, vases, and patterns, including Hull's famous Gingerbread Man.

Louise Bauer in her studio looking over molds of some of her designs that were not put into production before the Hull plant closed in 1986.

Photograph of a portion of Louise Bauer's designs stored on the second floor of her studio.

ACME

The Acme Pottery Company was formed in 1903 and began producing pieces until the Hull plant was formed in 1907.

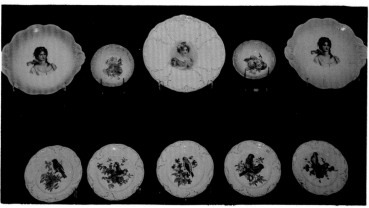

Row 1

1. Acme Porcelain Crooksville plate, scroll stamp, 11" $175
2. Acme Porcelain fruit bowl, eagle stamp, 5 1/2" $65
3. Acme Porcelain plate, eagle stamp, 10 1/2" $135
4. Acme Porcelain fruit bowl, eagle stamp, 5 1/2" $65
5. Acme Porcelain Crooksville plate, scroll stamp, 11" $175

Row 1

1. Acme covered casserole $125
2. Acme platter $175
3. Acme salad plate..$65
4. Acme soup bowl $65

ADVERTISING

The advertising signs are so rare that pricing is very difficult. It is a lucky collector who owns one of the three advertising pieces shown.

The small plaques are 5 1/2" x 2 1/4"and range from $3500 and up. The large plaque is 11" x 5 1/4" and ranges from $5000 and up.

Vary rare Little Red Riding Hood advertising plaque 12" x 6 1/2" around $25,000.

These ads ran in *"The Gift And Art Buyer"* magazine for May & June of 1945.

BLOSSOM FLITE

A pink high gloss and floral design with black or blue lattice markings decorate the Hull Blossom Flite pattern. Blossom Flite was produced by Hull in the middle 1950's.

Row 1
1. T1 6" honey jug $55
2. T2 6" basket $65
Page 12. T3 8 1/2" pitcher $125
3. T4 8 1/2" basket..$110

Row 2
1. T6 10 1/2" cornucopia..$90
2. T7 9 1/2" vase..$95
3. T8 8 1/4" x 9 1/4" basket...$125
NP. T9 10" low basket...$135

Row 3
1. T10 16 1/2" x 6 3/4" console bowl...........................$125
2. T11 3 1/4" candleholders pr...$75

Row 1
    1. T12 10 1/2" boat flower bowl $85
    2. T13 12 1/2" pitcher $150

Row 2
    1. T14 8" teapot...$95
    2. T15 creamer..$50
    3. T16 sugar (no lid) $50

Unusual plate & lazy susan pieces.

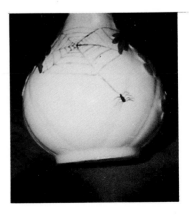

T 13 1/2" pitcher painted with spider web & spider.

CEREAL WARE

Cereal Ware was produced by Hull from 1915 to 1935, and was sold in sets or individually.

Canisters, each $100
Spice jars, each $75
Cruet, each.....................$150
Salt Box...........................$175

Top Photo
  Bluebird Cereal Ware

Middle Photo
  Delft Cereal Ware

Bottom Photo
  Conventional Rose Cereal Ware

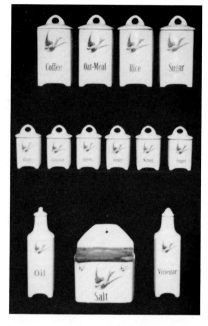

BOW KNOT

Manufactured in late forties, Bow Knot is a favorite in many collections. This matte-finished pattern is made in pastel pink/blue or turquoise/blue. Most pieces feature a ribbon bow.

Row 1
1. B-1 5 1/2" pitcher..$195
2. B-2 5" vase...$175
3. B-3 6 1/2" vase $200
4. B-4 6 1/2" vase $200
5. B-5 7 1/2" cornucopia $165
6. B-6 6 1/2" planter/saucer..$215

Row 2
1. B-7 8 1/2" vase $275
2. B-8 8 1/2" vase $275
3. B-9 8 1/2" vase $275
4. B-10 10 1/2" vase $475
5. B-11 10 1/2" vase $485

Row 3
1. B-12 10 1/2 basket...$750
2. B-13 13 1/2" double cornucopia $295
3. B-14 12 1/2" vase $1200
4. B-15 13 1/2" pitcher...$1300

Row 1
1. B-16 13 1/2" console bowl..$325
2. B-17 4" candleholders pr..$225
3. B-18 5 3/4" jardiniere..$200
4. B-19 9 3/8" jardiniere..$900

Row 2
1. B-20 6" teapot...$500
2. B-21 4" creamer...$175
3. B-22 4" sugar (lid missing)...$175
4. B-24 6" wall planter cup & saucer...........................$265
5. B-25 6 1/2" basket...$300

Row 3
1. B-26 6" wall planter pitcher.....................................$265
2. B-27 8" wall planter whisk broom............................$265
3. B-28 10" plate/plaque...$1200
4. B-29 12" basket..$2000
5. Unmarked wall pocket iron....................................$275

Rare B-2 painted in shades of tan and brown

The first B-1 vase is a reproduction. Notice it is slightly smaller and the design is not as clear as the original. Several Bow Knot pieces have been reproduced. It may pay the collector to buy carefully.

BUTTERFLY

The Hull Butterfly pattern was manufactured in the middle 1950's. Colors were ivory smooth matte finish or white pebble effect, both featuring pink, black, and blue butterflies.

Row 1
1. B1 6" pitcher $45
2. B2 6" small cornucopia...$40
3. B3 7" ashtray..$55
4. B4 6" bon bon dish...$40
5. B5 6" jardiniere...$50
6. B6 5 1/2" candy dish $50

Row 2
1. B7 9 3/4" rectangular bowl $50
2. B8 12 3/4" window box $50
3. B9 9" vase...$55
4. B10 7" vase..$55

Row 3
1. B11 8 3/4" pitcher..$115
2. B12 10 1/2" cornucopia..$80
3. B13 8" basket...$150

Row 1

1. B14 10 1/2" vase..$85
2. B15 13 1/2" Pitcher $185
3. B16 10 1/2" fruit bowl....................................$125
4. B17 10 1/2" basket $325
5. B24 lavabo top $100
6. B25 lavabo bottom $100

Row 2

1. B18 teapot...$150
2. B19 creamer...$50
3. B20 sugar with lid $50
4. B21 console bowl...$150
5. B22 candle holder..$35
6. B23 11 1/2" serving tray $150

CALLA LILY/JACK IN THE PULPIT

The Calla Lily design is often referred to as Jack-in-the Pulpit. It was manufactured in the late 1930's. The matte colors are in numerous shades of blues, yellows, greens, pinks, and rusts in various combinations.

Row 1
1. 500/32 8" bowl..$135
2. 500/32 10" bowl..$185
3. 500/33 6" vase..$110
4. 500/33 8" vase..$145
5. 501/33 6" vase..$125

Row 2
1. 502/33 6" vase..$110
2. 503/33 6" vase..$110
3. 504 6" vase..$125
4. 505 6" vase..$125
5. 506 10" pitcher...$330

Row 3
1. 510/33 8" vase..$145
2. 520/33 6" vase..$110
3. 520/33 8" vase..$150
4. 520/33 10" vase..$350
5. 530/33 5" vase..$100

Row 1

1. 530/33 7" vase $135
2. 530/33 9" vase $350
3. 540/33 6" vase $110
NP. 550/33 5" vase $110
4. 550/33 7 1/2" vase...$140
5. 560/33 10" vase $275
6. 560/33 13" vase $350

Row 2

1. 570/33 8" cornucopia $110
2. 591 7" jardiniere $300
3. 2 1/4" unmarked candleholders, pr........................$200
4. 590/33 13" x 4" console bowl..............................$325

Row 3

1. 592 6" flower pot...$125
2. 920/33 5" unknown design................................$50
3. 920/33 5" unknown design................................$50
4. 920/33 5" unknown design................................$50
5. 930/33 5" unknown design................................$50

CAPRI

Manufactured in the early 1960's, Capri has a rough texture. It is finished in shades of Coral or Seagreen.

NP. C14 4" vase $20
NP. C15 5 3/4" pedestal vase $25
NP. C21 3" swan planter $15
NP. C23 8 1/2" swan planter (See Page 53, Picture 3, Row 2, No.1) ..$35
NP. C28 9 3/4" vase..$40
NP. C29 12" vase $60
NP. C38 6 3/4" basket (See Page 41, Row 2, No.1) $30

Row 1
1. C44 4 1/4" jardiniere $20
NP. C45 4 1/4" x 6" ribbed pedestal flower bowl.............$20
2. C46 4 1/2" x 8" flower bowl...$25
3. C47 5 1/4" x 8" round flower bowl $30
NP. C47C 5 1/4" x 8" bon bon bowl (same as above with lid)......$40

Row 2
1. C48 12 1/4" x 5 1/2" basket...$45
2. C49 5 3/4" lion head goblet...$35
NP. C50 9" lion head goblet...$45
3. C52 10" x 7 1/2" ash tray $45
NP. C57 14 1/2" open front hanging
    basket vase (see page 24 No. C57) $85
NP. C58 13 3/4" vase..$75
NP. C59 15" vase $95
NP. C62 5 1/2" compote $25
NP. C62C 8 1/2" candy dish with lid (See Page 24 No. C62C) ...$35
4. C63 14" caladium leaf dish $75
NP. C67 4" square footed planter/candleholder $20
NP. C68 8 1/2" rectangular flower dish $30

Row 3
1. C80 llama planter $95
2. C81 twin swan planter..$65
3. C87 12" pine cone pitcher $95
NP. C314 flying duck planter $65

(*NP - not pictured)

Choose from three sizes of
Pitchers: 16-oz., 32-oz. and
2-qt. (Latter has ice lip.)

Capacious Salt, Pepper and
Grease Jar. Combined they
make a smart Range Set.

Cookie Jar is 10" deep, 7"
wide. Nested Mixing Bowls
in three deep, ample sizes.

Choose them with covers as
Casseroles, without covers as
Baking Dishes. 2 sizes.

Sugar, Creamer and Covered
Tea Pot. Can be purchased
individually or as Tea Set.

**THE A. E. HULL
POTTERY CO.**
CROOKSVILLE, OHIO

Cinderella is the trademark name for the kitchen items called Blossom with a single flower, and Bouquet with a pink, yellow, and blue flower. These items were manufactured late in the 1940's and into the 1950's.

Row 1
1. Pitcher - 16 oz. $25
2. Pitcher - 32 oz. $35
3. Pitcher - 2 qt. $45

Row 2
1. Salt shaker $15
2. Grease jar $50
3. Pepper shaker $15

Row 3
1. Cookie Jar $100
2. Bowls.....................$30, $40, $60

Row 4
1. Casserole $50
2. Casserole $60

Row 5
1. Creamer $15
2. Tea Pot $95
3. Sugar...................................$15

This tea set was hand painted in 22 karat gold by Gladys Showers, (pictured), marked Hull 23-24-25.

CLASSIC

The classic line of Hull pottery was manufactured for chain store use in the 1950's. Classic colors were glossy pink or ivory over a rough surface with a single pink or blue flower.

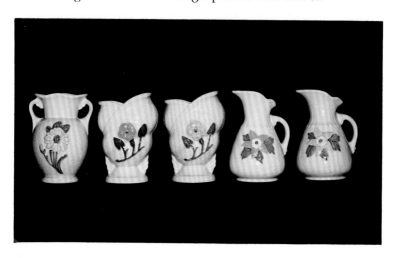

Row 1

1. 4-6" vase $25
2. & 3. 5-6" vases $25
4. & 5. 6-6" pitchers..$25

Make This Note for the Future:

When Victory is won and full production can be resumed, this trade mark of the "Potter-at-Wheel" will appear on Art Pottery of revolutionary design and color. Today's planning of the A. E. Hull Pottery Company, at Crooksville, Ohio, is destined to achieve that end.

By Any Name—

Hull Art Pottery would still have what it has—character, beauty and integrity of workmanship. The association of these qualities with the name of Hull is why we remind you to buy by the MARK!

A.E. Hull Pottery Co.
CROOKSVILLE, OHIO

These ads ran in *"The Gift And Art Buyer"* magazine.

CLOCKS

One of the liveliest topics of conversation by avid Hull collectors may center around the Bluebird and other clocks with movements by Sessions. I was pleased to meet Don Whitehouse, who was employed at the Hull factory from 1937-40. Mr. Whitehouse informed me that he had worked on several clocks during that time, and that they were, indeed, manufactured by Hull.

Previous information sent to this author was that the Hull company received the order from a New York based company to make the clocks. Unable to produce the shells in such volume at that time, the making of the molds was sublet to a Chicago company. The Hull company painted and assembled the clocks with Sessions movements, and filled the order for the New York company.

Many feel that Hull never made the clocks and Pam Curran, Shawnee's newsletter publisher, and Mark Supnick, author of *Collecting Shawnee Pottery*, have been researching to see if Shawnee did make these clocks. If not Hull or Shawnee, who made these lovely clocks? In the meantime, collectors of both potteries continue to add them to their collections and hope factual evidence will be found to definitely prove their origin.

The clocks seem to be more prevalent than originally thought by the owner of the clocks pictured on this page. Therefore buyers have found them from "dirt cheap" to $500.00.

This clock was designed and made at the Hull plant in the late 40's by Burley Channel.

Bluebird clock by Sessions painted in the brilliant shades of Hull's Little Red Riding Hood items.

CONTINENTAL

Continental is a very modern pottery, manufactured in the late 1950's with high gloss finish and stripes. Continental is in three colors: Evergreen, Persimmon and Mountain Blue.

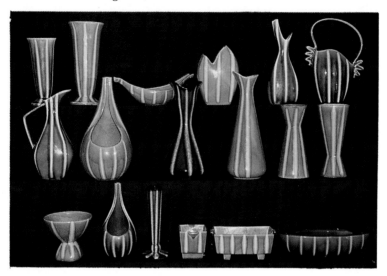

Row 1

NP. A1 8" ash tray	$40
NP. A3 12" rectangular ash tray	$65
NP. A20 10" ash tray with pen	$55
1. C28 9 3/4" vase	$55
2. C29 12" vase	$95
3. C51 15 1/2" x 3 1/4" flower dish	$65
NP. C52 10" x 7 1/4" ash tray	$65
4. C53 8 1/2" vase	$50
5. C54 12 1/2" vase	$75
6 C55 12 1/2" basket	$150

Row 2

1. C56 12 1/2" pitcher	$150
2. C57 14 1/2" open front (hanging basket) vase	$125
3. C58 13 3/4" vase	$100
4. C59 15" vase	$110
NP. C60 15" pedestal vase	$125
5. & 6. C61 10" vase/candleholders	$60

Row 3

1. C62 8 1/4" candy dish	$45
NP. C63 14" caladium leaf (see page 20, row 2)	$85
2. C64 10" open front vase (hanging basket)	$75
3. C66 9 1/2" bud vase	$45
4. C67 4" square planter/candleholder	$30
5. C68 8 1/2" x 4 1/2" rectangular planter	$30
NP. C69 9 1/4" footed flower bowl	$50
6. C70 13 1/4" console/candleholder bowl	$85

(*NP. - not pictured)

The Crab Apple design seems to be a difficult pattern for collectors to find. It was manufactured in the mid 1930's in 18 known molds of vases in shades of blue, tan, or white.

Row 1
1. 7" vase...$125
2. 7" vase...$105
3. 8" vase...$135
4. 8" vase...$135
5. 9" vase...$150

Row 2
1. 3" vase...$35
2. 4" vase...$45
3. 5" vase...$60
4. 6" vase...$75
5. 5" vase...$60

Row 3
1. 4" jardinere...$45
2. 6" jardinere...$75
3. 6 1/2" jardinere $80
4. 8" jardinere...$150

Row 4
1. 8 1/2" flower bowl..$175
2. 6" planter and saucer...$200
3. 6" hanging basket..$200
4. 7" hanging basket..$300

COOKIE JAR/BOY BLUE
No. 158 Cookie Jar - $450

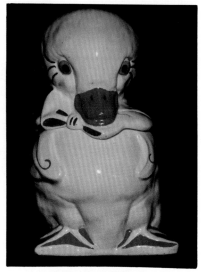

COOKIE JAR/DUCK
No. 966 Cookie Jar - $125

CRESCENT

Crescent kitchen items were made in the 1950's featuring crescent handles. Items were manufactured in shades of chartreuse/dark green and shades of brick/rose.

NP. B-1 5 1/2" bowl $10
NP. B-1 7 1/2" bowl $15
NP. B-1 9 1/2" bowl $20
Row 1
  1. B-2 10" casserole/lid $40
  NP. B-4 3 1/2" shaker $10
  NP. B-5 3 1/2" shaker $10
  2. B-7 5 1/2" casserole/lid .$20
  3. B-8 9 1/2" cookie jar/lid $65

Row 2
  1. B-13 7 1/2" teapot/lid....$65
  2. B-14 4 1/2" sugar/lid.....$20
  3. B-15 4 1/4" creamer........$20
  4. B-14 4 1/4" sugar/lid.....$20
  5. B-15 4 1/4" creamer........$20

Debonair oven proof kitchenware was made in the 1950's in stripes and shades of glossy pink and gray or in solid colors.

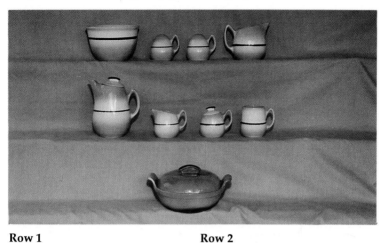

Row 1

1. 01 3 piece mixing bowl
   set (shown 7") ....$15,$25,$35
NP. 02 covered casserole.....$35
2. 04 salt shaker.....................$10
3. 05 pepper shaker $10
4. 06 pitcher $25
NP. 07 individual covered
   casserole $10
NP. 08 covered cookie jar....$50
NP. 010 cereal/salad bowl..$ 5

Row 2

1. 013 coffee/tea pot............$40
2. 014 creamer $10
3. 015 covered sugar............$10
4. 016 mug $10

Row 3

1. 017 partitioned dutch
   oven/cover $40

(*NP- not pictured)

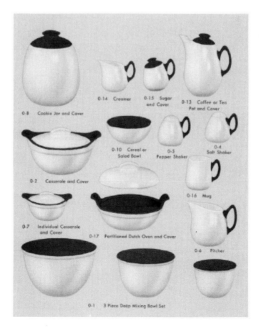

DOGWOOD/ WILD ROSE

Dogwood or Wild Rose, manufactured in the middle 1940's is one of the lovely matte finish designs. The vases come in shades of peach, pink/blue, or turquoise/peach.

Row 1
1. 501 7 1/2" basket..$300
2. 502 6 1/2" suspended vase..$225
3. 503 8 1/2" vase...$150

Row 2
1. 504 8 1/2" vase...$150
2. 505 7" pitcher..$275
3. 506 11 1/2" pitcher $350
4. 507 5 1/2" teapot & lid...$350

Row 3
1. 508 10 1/2" window box...$195
2. 509 6 1/2" vase...$125
3. 510 10 1/2" vase...$275

Row 1
1. 511 11 1/2" cornucopia $245
2. 512 4" candleholders pr. $125

Row 2
1. 513 6 1/2" vase..$125
2. 514 4" jardiniere $110
3. 515 8 1/2" vase..$175
4. 516 4 3/4" vase..$75
5. 517 4 3/4" vase..$75

Row 3
1. 519 13 1/2" pitcher $775
2. 520 4 3/4" pitcher $125
3. 521 7" low bowl...$150
4. 522 4" cornucopia $75

EBB TIDE

Manufactured in the middle 1950's, Ebb Tide shapes are of fish and shells in shades of chartreuse/wine and shrimp/turquoise.

Row 1

1. E-1 7" bud vase...$75
2. E-2 7" twin fish vase...$95
3. E-3 7 1/2" cornucopia with mermaid.....................$195
4. E-4 8 1/4" pitcher vase..$135
5. E-5 9 1/8" basket...$110
6. E-6 9 1/4" angel fish vase..$145
7. E-7 11" fish vase...$165

Row 2

1. E-8 ash tray with mermaid.......................................$195
2. E-9 11 3/4" cornucopia...$200
3. E-10 13" pitcher..$250
4. E-11 16 1/2" basket..$275

Row 3

1. E-12 15 3/4" snail console bowl..............................$185
2. E-13 candleholders pr...$95
3. E-14 teapot/lid...$195
4. E-15 creamer...$60
5. E-16 sugar/lid..$60

FANTASY

Fantasy molds were made in the late 1950's in pink, blue, and black.
Some pieces are finished with a foam edge.

Row 1
1. small rectangular planter $20
2. 19 very large heart-shaped
     ash tray planter............................$60
3. 35 rectangular planter...................$20
Row 2
1. 57 pedestal vase.............................$40

2. 73 vase 9 1/2" $45
3. 74 window box $45
Row 3
1. 76 pedestal planter $35
2. 77 pedestal fruit bowl $100
3. 78 tall candleholders.....................$65

FIESTA

A 1950's glossy decorated in fruits, flowers, animals and other designs.

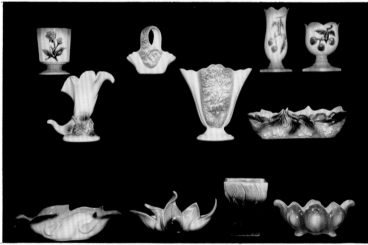

Row 1
1. 43 pedestal planter (rose design)...........$35
2. 44 basket (squirrel design) $30
3. 45 pedestal vase (strawberry design)..............$45
4. 46 pedestal planter (strawberry design)...$50
Row 2
1. 49 8 1/2" cornucopia (grape design).......$50

2. 50 vase (deer design)...............................$55
3. 52 12" planter (leaves and berries) $45
Row 3
1. 78 12" leaf shaped planter $55
2. 112 10" leaf and grape wall planter ...$45
3. 116 6" rectangular vase with leaves..$35
4. 403 scalloped planter............................$45

FLORAL

Floral is a kitchen ware line manufactured in the early 1950's featuring a yellow sunflower or daisy type flower.

Row 1

1. 40 5" mixing bowl...$10
2. 40 6" mixing bowl...$15
3. 40 7" mixing bowl...$20
4. 40 8" mixing bowl...$25
5. 40 9" mixing bowl...$30
NP. 41 9" lipped mixing bowl...$40
NP. 42 7 1/2" covered casserole $40
NP. 43 5 3/4" covered grease dish $35

Row 2

1. 44 3 1/2" salt & pepper...$25
2. 46 1 quart pitcher $40
NP. 47 casserole with lid..$45
3. 48 8 1/4" cookie jar and lid $50
4. 49 10" salad bowl...$45
NP. 50 6" cereal bowl ....$ 5

(*NP. - not pictured)

#79 6 1/2" basket - $65

GRANADA/MARDI GRAS

Granada/Mardi Gras vases were designed for ten cent store sales. Manufactured in the 1940's and 1950's. The vases are white, shades of pink/blue, or tans that have embossed flowers

Row 1
1. 31 10" pitcher $115
2. 32 8" basket $125
3. 33 5 1/2" teapot $200

Row 2
1. 47 9" vase.....................................$45
2. 48 9" vase.....................................$45
3. 49 9" vase.....................................$45

Row 3
1. 62-8" Morning Glory basket $425
2. 66-11" Morning Glory pitcher $425
3. 65-8" basket...............................$125
4. 66-10" pitcher...........................$125
5. 215-9" vase $45

61 - 9" Morning Glory vase - $200

219 - 9" vase - $45

Dinnerware prices are on pages 52 & 53.

Avocado kitchenware pieces were manufactured in 1968-1971. House & Garden molds were used to make the Heritageware pieces.

AVOCADO *with Ivory trim*

666 Pie Plate 9¼" Dia.	624 Ind. Bean Pot w/Cover 12 oz.	610 Bean Pot w/Cover 2 qt.	699 Luncheon Plate 9⅝" Dia.

698 Saucer 5⅝"	697 Cup 7 oz.	651 Jam or Mustard Jar w/Cover Set w/Spoon 12 oz.	661 Covered Butter Dish (¼ lb. Capacity)	674 Oval Bake 'n Serve Dish 10" x 5" x 1¾"

624-4 Beer Stein 16 oz.
4 Piece Party Pack Set
(Individual Carton 6 Sets to Master)

604—Oven Proof 16 Piece Starter Set

4 - Fruits—5¼"
4 - Mugs—9 oz.
4 - Salad Plates—6½"
4 - Dinner Plates—10¼" Dia.

670—Oven Proof 16 Piece Starter Set

4 - Fruits—6"
4 - Cups—7 oz.
4 - Saucers—5⅞"
4 - Luncheon Plates—9⅝" Dia.

Dinnerware prices are on pages 52 & 53.

The Spread Eagle pattern appearing on several shapes is an American symbol implying strength and character which is consistent with Dinnerware expected to withstand constant daily use both in and out of doors. Dinnerware prices are on pages 52 & 53.

an

ovenproof

creation

| 300 Dinner Plate 10¼" | 301 Salad or Dessert Plate 7½" | 302 Coffee Mug 9 oz. | 303 Fruit 6" | 304 Bread and Butter Plate 6½" | 305 Carafe w/Cover (2 Cup) |

hull pottery company —

| 306 Open Baker 32 oz. | 307 Casserole w/Cover 32 oz. | 308 Indiv. Casserole w/Cover 9 oz. | 310 Gravy Boat or Syrup 10 oz. 312 Two Piece Gravy Boat Set | 311 Saucer For Gravy Boat or Syrup 6½" | 313 French Handled Casserole 9 oz. |

crooksville, ohio u.s.a.

| 314 Custard Cup 6 oz. | 315 Salt Shaker 3¾" 316 Pepper Shaker 3¾" 317 Salt and Pepper Set | 318 Creamer 8 oz. | 319 Sugar Bowl w/Cover 8 oz. 320 Sugar and Creamer Set | 321 Chip 'n Dip Leaf 14¼"x10¼"x2¼" | 322 Coffee Server w/Cover (8 Cup) |

Dinnerware prices are on pages 52 & 53.

COUNTRY (BLUE) BELL

The Country Bell used the same molds as Heartland and has the Blue Bell flower motif. Prices are also similar to Heartland prices.

COUNTRY SQUIRE

The green agate pieces in the Rainbow pattern were given the name Country Squire when used in a setting of all green agate pieces.

Dinnerware prices are on pages 52 & 53.

The
Heartland
Collection

436 6" Bowl   438 8" Bowl   440 10" Bowl

Dinnerware prices are on pages 52 & 53.

HERITAGEWARE

Heritageware was made in mint green, azure blue, and yellow.

Grease jar - $35; Pitcher - $35; Pitcher - $35.

Salt & pepper on napkin rack - $50.

MARCREST

Hull manufactured dinnerware for Marcrest in the late 1950's in colors of green, pink, yellow, coral & white.

Row 1
1-3. nested mixing bowls $15, $25, $35
Row 2
1-4. mugs 3 3/4" $15
5. cocoa pot 11" $65

Dinnerware prices are on pages 52 & 53.

20

HERITAGEWARE & MARCREST

40

Manufactured in 1981-1985 in grey, brown, and sand.

Dinnerware prices are on pages 52 & 53.

New Addition to Hull's Famous Ovenproof

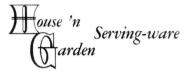

House 'n Garden Serving-ware

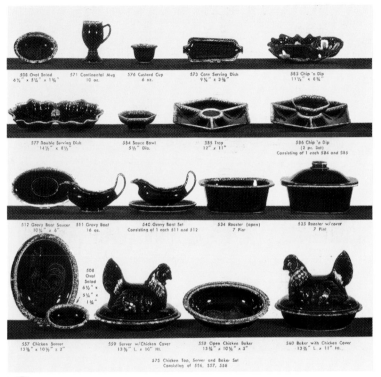

 hull pottery company — crooksville, ohio *u.s.a.*

Dinnerware prices are on pages 52 & 53.

*New Addition to Hull's Famous Ovenproof

House 'n Garden Serving-ware

529 Cup - 6 oz.
530 Saucer - 5½"
531 Luncheon Plate - 8½" Dia.

532 — 12 Piece Luncheon Set

4—Cups - 6 oz.
4—Saucers - 5½"
4—Luncheon Plates - 8½" Dia.

536 Mixing Bowl 6"

537 Mixing Bowl 7"

538 Mixing Bowl w/Pouring Spout 8"

539—3 Pc. Mixing Bowl Set (6", 7", 8")

*572 Jumbo Stein 32 oz.

*574 Oval Serving Dish 10" x 2" x 1¾"

590 Indl. Leaf Dish 7¾" x 4¾"

591 Leaf Shaped Chip 'n Dip 12½" x 9"

*592 Hen on Nest Casserole

*195 Corky Piggy Bank Mirror Brown Trimmed in Blue

*195 Corky Piggy Bank Mirror Brown Trimmed in Pink

*196 Sitting Piggy Bank Mirror Brown Trimmed in Yellow & Turquoise

*197 Jumbo Corky Piggy Bank Mirror Brown Trimmed in Yellow & Turquoise

hull pottery company — crooksville, ohio *u.s.a.*

Dinnerware prices are on pages 52 & 53.

504 16 Pc. Starter - Consists of 1 each: 500, 501, 302, 503

Dinnerware prices are on pages 52 & 53.

5439 — Consists of 1 each; 5436, 5438, 5440

Dinnerware prices are on pages 52 & 53.

Often the apple cookie jar, grease jar, and salt and pepper set have been reported as manufactured by Hull.

Red plaidware dishes owned by Charles Endres.

Relish plates - $125

Skillet tray - $125

Production of the orchid pitcher was just beginning when the plant closed.

HOUSE & GARDEN

Row 1

This 4 piece train canister set was produced during the final days of the Hull factory. The HULL POTTERY newsletter reports that only a few sets were completed and the train set is bound to be a special item for collectors. Prices are being quoted at $3000 and up a set.

Row 2

Gingerbread men cookie jars:
1. Grey $400
2. Original brown cookie jar (white clay) $150
3. Tan $500

The depot cookie jar was designed by Louise Bauer as a companion piece to the train set, but was not put into production before the factory closed. In 1992 Larry Taylor, president of the Hull Pottery Company, produced a limited number of these depots valued at $250. The advertising plaque was a souvenir sold at the Ohio Ceramic Center in 1992.

Dinnerware prices are on pages 52 & 53.

RAINBOW *by Hull* — LUNCHEON SET Illustrated

#232—12 pc.
Plate 8½"
Cup 6 oz.
Saucer 5½"

Mirror Brown   Butterscotch   Green Agate   Tangerine

Complete set also available in choice of each color shown—see list.

Also available in the four colors shown above.

No. 590 Individual
Leaf Dish 7¼" x 4¾"

No. 591 Leaf Shape
Chip 'n Dip 12¼" x 9"

No. 592 Two Tier Tidbit
Tray Set

Here is a new Mixing Bowl Set added
to Hull's Famous line of House 'n Garden
Serving and Kitchen Ware

No. 539—3 pc.
Mixing Bowl Set
(6"—7"—8")

No. 538 Mixing
Bowl w/Pouring
Spout 8"

No. 537
Mixing Bowl 7"

No. 536
Mixing Bowl 6"

Mixing Bowls and Serv-all Trays sold *only*
in Mirror Brown and Tangerine.

The complete line of House 'n Garden is available in Mirror
Brown or Tangerine, each trimmed in Ivory Foam . . . See list
for other items also offered in "Rainbow" assorted colors.

No. 540 Serv-All
Leaf Tray 12"x7½"

Dinnerware prices are on pages 52 & 53.

Flint Ridge

12 pc. Set
4 ea. Dinner Plate, Bowl, Mug

16 pc. Set
4 ea. DinnerPlate, Salad Plate, Bowl, Mug

Tawny Ridge

20 pc. Set
4 ea. Dinner Plate, Salad Plate, Bowl,
Cup, Saucer

Completer Set
1 ea. Sugar w/Cover, Creamer,
Vegetable Bowl, Steak Plate

Walnut Ridge

**Sugar &
Creamer Set**

**Salt &
Pepper Set**

6 pc. Snack Set
2 ea. Tray, Bowl, Mug

Centennial

Bean Pot w/cover, 7" x 9" $125
Casserole, 4 1/2 x 11" $125
Cereal Bowl, 5 3/4" (Unmarked)....$50
Creamer, 4 1/2" (Unmarked) $50
Milk Pitcher, 7 1/2" (Unmarked) ..$125
Mug, 4" (Unmarked) $50
Pepper Shaker, 3" (Unmarked) $30
Salt Shaker, 3" (Unmarked) $30
Stein, (32 Oz.) $55
Sugar Bowl, 3 3/4" $50

Dinnerware

Ash Tray w/Deer imprint, 8" $25
Bake 'n Serve Dish, Oval,
  9 1/2 Oz., (1980's) $10
Bake 'n Serve Dish, Oval, 16 Oz. $15
Bake 'n Serve, Round, 6 1/2" $10
Baker, Open (Rooster Imprint),
  3" Deep $50
Baker, Oval w/Chicken cover,
  13" x 11" $125
Baker, Rectangular (1980's) $30
Baker, Rectangle 7 Pt. Open $50
Baker, Square, 3 Pt. $15
Bean Pot w/cover, indv. 12 Oz. $5
Bean Pot w/cover, 2 Qt. $35
Beer Stein, 16 Oz. $10
Bud Vase, 9" $20
Butter Dish, Covered, 1/4 lb. $10
Canister, (Coffee)........................$75
Canister, (Flour) $75
Canister, (Sugar) $75
Canister Set, 4-piece Stacking,
  (1980's) $200
Canister, (Tea) $75
Carafe, 2 Cup...............................$30
Casserole, Open, Fr. Handled,
  9 Oz. $5
Casserole, Open, Fr. Handle Indv.
  (1980's) $5
Casserole, Oval, 2 Pt., 10" x 7 1/4",
  Open $15
Casserole w/Chicken cover,
  Oval, 2 Qt. $75
Casserole w/cover, Fr. Handled,
  9 Oz. (New) $10
Casserole w/cover, Fr. Handle Indv.
  (1980's) $10
Casserole w/cover, Oval, 2 Pt......$25
Casserole w/cover, Oval, 2 Qt. $35
Casserole w/cover, Round
  (1980's) $20
Casserole w/Duck cover,
  Oval, 2 Pt. $75

Casserole w/lid & warmer,
  Fr. Handled, 3 Pt. $100
Casserole w/lid, 32 Oz. $25
Cheese Server $25
Cheese Shaker $30
Chicken Cover Top for
  Baker/Platter $65
Chip 'n Dip, 2 pieces, 12" x 11" ..$125
Chip 'n Dip (3 Sections) $50
Chip 'n Dip Leaf, 12 1/4" x 9" $25
Chip 'n Dip Leaf, 15" x 10 1/2" $25
Chip 'n Dip, Sauce Bowl...............$65
Chip 'n Dip Set, Tray $55
Coffee Cup, 6 Oz. $5
Coffee Cup, 7 Oz. $5
Coffee Cup, (Mug), 9 Oz. $5
Coffee Pot, 8 Cup.........................$35
Condiment Set $125
Continental Mug, 10 Oz. & 12 Oz. $10
Cookie Jar w/cover, 94 Oz. $40
Corky Pig Bank $75
Corky Piggy Bank, Jumbo $125
Corn Serving Dish, 9 1/4" x 3 3/8"....$50
Creamer or Jug, 8 Oz./10 Oz. $10
Custard Cup, 6 Oz. $5
Custard Cup, 8 Oz. $10
Deviled Egg Server
  w/Rooster Imprint........................$50
Dinner Plate, 10 1/4" $10
Dutch Oven (2) Pieces, 3 Pt. $35
Fish Platter, 11" $50
Fruit Bowl, 5 1/4" $5
Fruit Bowl, 6" $5
Garlic Cellar, 13 Oz. (1980's)........$15
Gravy Boat & Saucer $35
Hen on Nest, Oval $75
Ice Jug, 2 Qt. $30
Jam/Mustard Jar w/cover,
  12 Oz. $10
Jam/Mustard Jar w/cover,
  13 Oz., (1980's) $10
Jug, 2 Pt. $20
Leaf Dish, Indv., 7 1/4" x 4 1/4" $10
Leaf Serve-All 12" x 7 1/2" $50
Luncheon Plate, 8 1/2" $10
Luncheon Plate, 9 3/8" $10
Mixing Bowl, 6"............................$10
Mixing Bowl, 7"............................$15
Mixing Bowl, 8"............................$20
Mug, 10 Oz. (1980's) $5
Oil Server $25
Onion Soup Bowl w/cover, 12 Oz.
  (1980's) $10
Pepper Shaker/Mushroom, 3 3/4"....$10
Pie Plate, 9 1/2" Dia. $25
Platter w/Chicken cover $125

Platter w/Rooster Imprint, Oval $50
Quiche Dish (1980's) $35
Ramekin, 2 1/2 Oz. (1980's) $10
Roaster, Rectangle w/cover, 7 Pt. $125
Salad Bowl, 10 1/4" $35
Salad Bowl w/Rooster imprint,
   oval...$15
Salad Plate, 6 1/2" $5
Salad Server, Rectangular,
   11" x 6 1/2".................................$25
Salt & Pepper Set,
   (Table Size) Set $25
Salt Shaker/Mushroom, 3 3/4" $10
Salt Shaker w/cork, 3 3/4" $5
Saucer, 5 1/2" $5
Saucer, 5 7/8" $5
Server, Handled $100
Serving Dish/Scalloped, Double ..$50
Serving Set $125
Sitting Pig Bank $75
Skillet, Handled $50-150
Souffle Dish, (1980's)...................$40
Soup Mug, 11 Oz. & 14 Oz. $10
Soup or Salad Bowl, 6 1/2" $5
Spaghetti Bowl, 10 1/4" $35
Spaghetti, Indv., Oval,
   10 3/4" x 8 1/4" $15
Spoon Rest/oval
   "Spoon Rest" imprint $25
Steak Plate, Indv. Oval,
   11 3/4" x 9" $10
Stein, Jumbo 32 Oz. $40
Sugar Bowl w/cover, 12 Oz. $10
Teapot & Lid.................................$35
Teapot w/cover, 5 Cup $35
Tidbit, Two-Tiered $35
Tray for Snack Set $10
Vegetable Dish, Divided,
   10 3/4" x 71/4" $20
Vinegar Server $20
Water Jug, 5 Pt. 80 Oz. $35
Well 'n Tree Steak Plate, Oval
   14" x 10" $40

Gingerbread

Gingerbread Depot Cookie Jar ..$275
Gingerbread Man/Child's Bowl....$150
Gingerbread Man/Child's Cup $125
Gingerbread Man Coaster
   5" x 5" $30
Gingerbread Man
   Cookie Jar/Brown......................$200
Gingerbread Man
   Cookie Jar/Gray $400
Gingerbread Man
   Cookie Jar/Sand........................$500

Gingerbread Man Server
   10" x 10" $75
Gingerbread Serving Tray $75
Gingerbread Train Caboose........$800
Gingerbread Train Coal Car........$800
Gingerbread Train Engine $800
Gingerbread Train
   Passenger Car $800
Gingerbread Train Set,
   Brown ....$3000 & up (set)
Vinegar Cruet, 5 3/4" $40

* The prices on these pages are only
suggested prices. Some patterns and
colors may be higher priced than
listed.

IMPERIAL, NOVELTY & MISC.

Imperial has been manufactured since the 1960's. The production of Imperial and other miscellaneous patterns is so extensive it is difficult to catalog. The Imperial section will therefore include many miscellaneous items produced not only under the Imperial name but one will also find Athena, Regal, Floraline, Royal and others. They are pictured in numerical order for the reader's convenience. This section also includes groupings of birds and fowl, animals, Madonnas, and other human figures.

Row 1
1. F1 green fan ....$ 5
2. B2 planter-mushroom design.....................................$10
3. F2 goblet planter ....$ 5
4. A3 square planter - leaf design ....$ 5
5. F3 goblet planter ....$ 5
6. A4 rectangular planter $10

Row 2
1. 5 Tokay jardiniere $20
2. F5 gold trimmed goblet..$10
3. A6 free form planter $10
4. B6 7" bow $10
5. F6 pedestal plate $10

Row 3
1. F8 pedestal bowl $10
2. F9 oval planter..$ 5
3. F10 round bowl ....$ 5
4. F11 rectangular planter ....$ 5

Row 1
   1. 56 Parchment & Pine basket...$35
   2. F56 wheeled white planter $10
   3. F63 goblet with leaf design...$10

Row 2
   1. F70 12" green bulb vase $25
   2. 71 Parchment & Pine console bowl $20
   3. 72 8" pedestal vase...$20
   4. 72 8" flowered see-through vase $50

Row 3
   1. 73 10" bird see-through vase with gold trim.............$50
   2. F77 oval planter..$15
   3. 78 9" bird vase..$65

A-50 pitcher - $45

Praying hands F475 - $50. Blossom Flite teapot T14 8" - $90, swirl pitcher F482-11" - $50, cornucopia F-479 6 5/8" $35 all in tangerine.

Row 1

1. 82 12" Fantasy window box $25
2. 83 Mayfair hand vase with 23 Karat gold trim $35
3. 85 large leaf shaped flat bowl...................................$25
4. 88 console bowl and candleholder (consolette)........$25

Row 2

1. F89 9" square vase $20
2. 91 console bowl and candleholder (consolette)........$35
3. F91 5" pitcher with eagle design $20
4. 92 7" planter with black flowers...............................$50

Row 3

1. 94 large bucket...$75
2. B94 bucket 9"..$45
3. F95 8" round footed bowl...$15
4. F96 rectangular planter $10

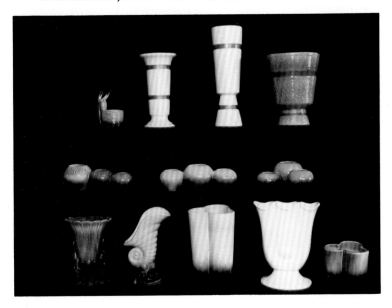

Row 1

1. 101 wishing well planter...$25
2. 102 12" gold banded vase...$35
3. 104 15" gold banded vase...$50
4. 105 8 1/2" gold banded vase......................................$50

Row 2

1. 105 triple bulb planter...$25
2. 106 triple bulb planter 10 1/2".....................................$25
3. 107 triple bulb planter...$25

Row 3

1. 108 Woodland suspended vase....................................$60
2. 108 Athena shell cornucopia 8 1/2".............................$35
3. 110 9" triple vase...$35
4. 112 10" triple vase...$40
5. 121 5" triple vase...$20

Row 1
1. 150 pedestal planter..$ 5
2. 151 free form window box...$25
3. 152 free form window box...$25
4. 153 Fantasy rectangular window box 12 1/2"..........$30

Row 2
1. 156 pedestal planter...$20
2. 157 pedestal rectangular planter $20
3. 158 square candy dish with lid $40
4. 159 pedestal fruit bowl...$50

Row 3
1. 161 8" vase $15
2. 162 11" vase $35
3. 163 12" vase $35
4. 201 shell cornucopia $25
5. 203 shell cornucopia $25

Heart ash tray &
planter - $100

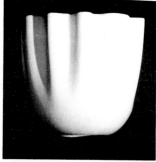

Hull 427 9 1/2" x 10 1/2" large
white planter - $75. (Was
originally in wire holder.)

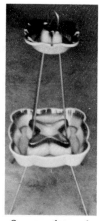

Square ash tray &
planter- $100

Row 1
1. 307 Regal shell cornucopia $25
2. 401 rectangular planter $10
3. 402 rectangular planter $25
4. 407 Floraline ribbed goblet $10
5. 415 Snail shell cornucopia $35

Row 2
1. 418 5" jardiniere $15
2. 419 6" jardiniere $25
3. 450 cart rectangular planter..$10
4. F467 ribbed rectangular planter...................................$10
5. F469 ribbed rectangular planter...................................$10

Row 3
1. 491 goblet $10
2. 530 clock planter (not Hull) $50
3.   conch shell..$35
4.   silver goblet with 4 faces (not Hull) $50
5.   ash tray unicorn design..$40

The Athena oval picture frame wall planters are marked 611 USA. The square frame has no number. $125 each.

Row 1
1.   cat/kitten lamp $95
2. 61 cat/kitten basket planter...$50
3. 89 cat/kitten & spool planter $50
4. 38 dog/poodle hat planter $65
5. 114 poodle base $50
6. 119 15" dog/dachshund planter...........................$110

Row 2
1. 57 9" deer planter...$60
2. 62 12" deer planter...$85
3. 115 9" giraffe planter $45
4.   horse/colt dish planter $75
5. 965 lamb planter...$65

Row 3
1. 39 pig planter..$65
2. 196 House & Garden sitting pig $75
3.   Corky pig bank..$75
4. 98 10" unicorn vase...$50
5. 98 12" unicorn vase...$75

Novelty items: pig, deer, pig planter No. 86, cat and cat. Prices may run from $25 to $125.

(ANIMALS)

The man on the donkey figurine was made at the Hull Pottery Company and sent to President Franklin D. Roosevelt during WWII. The donkey represents the democratic party.

Row 1 Male/Female turnabout cat 11" - $95; Cat vase 809 11" - $125.
Row 2 Teddy Bear Planter 811 7" - $45; Siamese cats 63 5 3/4" - $85.

The poodle & kitten planters in matte finish are usually found in gloss - $150 each.

The bank on the right is marked hull USA 107 and is much larger than the more common corky pig.

The rabbit candy dish is a Hull experimental piece that was never put into full production.

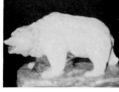

Bear dated 1931 was photographed at the Hull convention at Crooksville, Ohio in 1992.

Only a few lions were produced. This lion belonged to Greg Garrett. $1000.

IMPERIAL, NOVELTY & MISC. - continued
(ANIMALS)

Most of the items on this page were photographs from the extensive Higginbotham collection.

This collection of multi-colored corky pigs is part of the Higginbotham collection. $50-$150.

Unicorn 119, Teddy Bear 811 USA, Rabbit Imperial F15, Pig Barrel. $50 to $100.

Monkeys & Elephants $75.

Double hippo 81, larger hippo F68, small hippo 83. $75 to $175.

Turtle, fish planter, fish, and aquatic frog. $50 to $75.

Row 1
1. 405 bird $15
2. F473 chickadee..$20
3. 53 chicken/rooster $35
4. 95 House & Garden chicken/rooster $100

Row 2
1. 74 bandanna duck $50
2. 75 bandanna duck $35
3. 76 bandanna duck $25
4. 77 bandanna duck candleholder $60
5. 540 flying duck wall planter $95

Row 3
1. 67 flying goose wall planter $45
2. 94 twin geese..$30
3. 95 twin geese..$50
4. 231E goose planter $50
5. 411 Jubilee long neck goose $65
6. 41 long neck goose $25

Goose F471, Penguin hull F472, Rooster 951 USA. $50 to $75.

Handled goose basket No. 413 - $75. Penguin planter is F472 - $75.

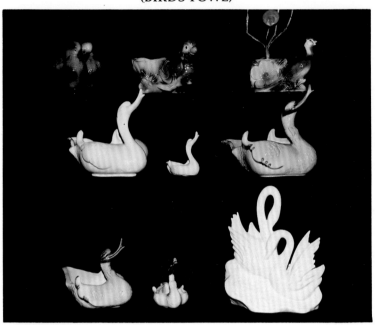

Row 1
1. 93 Royal love birds $40
2. 60 parrot planter $50
3. 61 pheasant planter $50

Row 2
1. F23 Capri swan $50
2. F21 Capri swan $15
3. 69 swan $50

Row 3
1. 80 swan $30
2. swan $20
3. 81 double swan $75

Small flying duck 79 - $65. Large flying duck 10 1/2" 104 - $95.

This bird flower frog is a rare item in Hull's designs. The bird flower frog 10 1/2" is $95. The 13" low flower bowl base is number 85 for $50.

Row 1
1. tulip shaped lamp...$95
2. 24 Madonna $35
3. 25 Madonna $35

Row 2
1. 26 Madonna $35
2. 27 standing Madonna...$50
3. F61 Madonna $45
4. 81 standing Madonna...$45

Row 3
1. 89 Saint Francis..$65
2. 204 Madonna $35
3. 417 Madonna $60

BAND MEMBERS

Band members sell for $150 each.

Row 1
1. 92 baby & pillow planter..............$25
2. 62 child planter $30

Row 2
1. 120 Chinese man wall planter $75
2. 82 clown planter $55
3. 90 little girl planter.......................$25

Row 3
1. 55 knight on horse planter $85
2. 954 lady & basket planter.............$40
3. 955 dancing lady planter.............$50

Farmer Boy Planter #91 - $50.

Girl Planter 87 USA Chinaman Hull 120, Imperial Cherub girl head planter, girl head in bonnet. $50 to $125.

Coronet queen with crown #209 - 9", $95.

The Iris (Narcissus) pattern was produced in as many as four sizes for each mold, making it interesting for the collector to search for each size. Manufactured in the middle 1940's, Iris is found in colors of peach, pink/blue, and shades of rose/peach.

Row 1
1. 401-5" pitcher..$100
2. 401-8" pitcher..$250
3. 401-13 1/2" pitcher $475
4. 402-4 3/4" vase...$75
5. 402-7" vase $125
6. 402-8 1/2" vase..$150

Row 2
1. 403-4 3/4" vase...$80
2. 403-7" vase $140
3. 403-8 1/2" vase..$175
4. 403-10 1/2" vase..$325
5. 404-4 3/4" vase...$80
6. 404-7" vase $155
7. 404-8 1/2" vase..$150
8. 404-10 1/2" vase..$325

Row 3
1. 405-4 3/4" vase...$80
2. 405-7" vase $125
3. 405-8 1/2" vase..$175
4. 405-10 1/2" vase..$325
5. 406-4 3/4" vase...$80
6. 406-7" vase $125
7. 406-8 1/2" vase..$150
NP. 406-10 1/2" vase...$325

Row 1
1. 407-4 3/4" vase..$80
2. 407-7" vase...$125
3. 407-8 1/2" vase..$150
4. 408-7" basket...$325

Row 2
1. 409-12" console bowl..$225
2. 410-7 1/2" bud vase..$145
3. 411-5" candleholders pr. $175

Row 3
1. 412-4" hanging basket planter $85
2. 412-7" hanging basket planter $175
3. 413-5 1/2" jardiniere..$145
4. 413-9" jardiniere...$350
5. 414-10 1/2" vase...$350
6. 414-16" floor vase...$600

Hull, it seems, was never in the lamp business, but a number of lamp bases seem to show up and are considered as employee specials made for gifts or their own personal use. Factory made lamps demand a higher price then the homemade lamps made from Hull vases.

1. lamp base, unnamed design, L-1, 12 3/4" $500
2. lamp base, Classic design, unmarked 7 3/4" $200
3. lamp base, Orchid, 303, 10" $600
4. lamp base, unnamed design, 9", USA No. 1...........$600
5. lamp base, Rosella, L-3, 11" $400

Row 1
  1. tulip shaped lamp $95
  2. kitten planter $95
  3. pheasant planter..$75
Row 2
  1. Little Red Riding Hood lamp....................................$2800
  2. Rosella lamp 6 3/4"...$235
  3. Tulip lamp..$600

Rare Tulip lamp base, 100-3-6 1/2" $600; 107-33-10" $800; 107-33-6 1/2" $700.

Woodland Candleholder Lamps, pair - $500

1. Water Lily Lamp - $450.
2. Woodland Teapot Lamp - $500

A "one-of a kind" lamp designed and pre-scented to the original owner. He shared this beautiful lamp with the Hull collectors at the First Annual Hull convention in 1992 in Crooksville, Ohio.

Lovely Magnolia tasseled vase 21" x 12 1/2" lamp - $500.

Pair of Bow Knot B-4 lamps - $400 each.

Iris 414 16" - $750

Employee specialty Waterlily lamp in a rare shade of green - $500

Novelty Lamp - $600

Three Hull lamps: Orchid 302 10", Woodland, and Orchid 302 4 3/4".

Orchid 302 8" lamp, and a L-2 lamp made at Hull plant and decorated by Ard Richards for Harvey Allen.

TV lamps made from Ebbtide basket E11-16 1/2", and console E12-15 3/4".

Dachshund planter lamp. Paul Trussell, Hull plant worker, designed and made the two bear lamps.

LEEDS

The pig and elephant liquor bottles were produced by Hull for the Leeds Company in the middle 1940's. The pig and the elephant are 7 3/4". Prices vary widely on Leeds items. Prices are cheaper near Crooksville, Ohio and surrounding states and appear to be much higher the further away you are. I have been quoted prices from $40 to $165.

Pig banks, 5".

Leeds pig lamp.

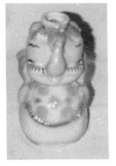

This yellow elephant was rescued floating down the river during the flood and fire that destroyed the Hull Plant in 1950. It was photographed in Louise Bauer's studio.

The Little Red Riding Hood items were produced in the late 1950's with several markings. Many are marked Little Red Riding Hood, Pat-Des-No-135889 U.S.A. Others bear the number 967. Blank molds were sold to and decorated by Royal & Regal. Other companies have claimed they produced many of the Little Red Riding Hood items using the poppy decal that Hull used for decorating.

Row 1
1. advertising plaque...$25,000
2. baby feeding dish...$8000-$8500
3. baby or chocolate mug.......................................$2500-$3000
4. wall bank..$3300
5. standing bank...$750

Row 2
1. butter dish.....................$450
2. cereal canister.............$1250
3. coffee canister...............$750
4. flour canister.................$750
5. popcorn canister.........$4000

Row 3
1. potato chip canister ...$4000
2. pretzel canister...........$4000
3. sugar canister................$750
4. salt canister.................$1250
5. tea canister....................$750

The cookies & peanuts canisters are very rare. $4000 each.

Row 1
1. small single decal $400
2. large single decal $400
3. two decals.................................$400
4. three decals...............................$400
5. four decals $500

Row 2
1. cold painted (varies by
     condition of paint).... $300-$1000
2. gold star apron/sprig
     border $500
3. gold star apron/scattered
     orange flowers.......................$400
4. gold star apron/2 sprig
     borders $400
5. gold star apron/4 decals $400

Row 3
1. gold bowed apron/red
     shoes & red spray $800
2. gold bowed apron/red
     shoes & red spray $800
3. closed basket, two decals $400
4. gold bowed apron, closed
     basket, 3 decals, red shoes........$500
5. green basket, poinsettia
     decals $1200

Rare 967 cookie jar with 5 pink roses and grey leaves - $800. The sticker reads:

Palette & Brushes
Hand Painted
Fired Ceramic Colors
22 Karat Gold

Row 1
    1. Little Red Riding Hood covered casserole.............$8000
    2. cracker jar..$750
    3. dresser/grease jar Hull Ware 982 USA $750
    4. lamp $2800
    5. match box for wooden matches................................$900

Row 2
    1. 5 1/2" mustard jar with spoon $475
    2. planter...$8500
    3. 9" wall pocket planter $550
    4. 6 1/2" batter pitcher $500
    5. 8" milk pitcher..$425

Row 3
    1-2. 3 1/2" small salt & pepper shakers.........................$85
    3-4. 4 1/2" medium salt & pepper shakers $1400
    5-6. 5" large salt & pepper shakers..............................$175
    7-8. 5 1/2" sitting salt & pepper shakers...................$2500

Row 1

1. stringholder $3300
2. allspice spice jar...$850
3. cinnamon spice jar $850
4. cloves spice jar...$850
5. ginger spice jar $850
6. nutmeg spice jar $850
7. pepper spice jar $850

Row 2

1. side pour sugar...$200
2. side pour creamer $200
3. crawling sugar..$325
4. tab handle creamer $325
5. sugar with lid $525
6. creamer with pantaloons $500

Row 3

1. teapot..$375
2. wolf grease jar, yellow $1100
3. wolf grease jar, red $1300

Vary rare Little Red Riding Hood pitcher.

1. LRRH's basket. 2. Unusually painted blank spice jar. 3 & 4. Rare blue and white small salt & pepper shakers. 5. Unusually painted middle sized salt & pepper shakers. 6. Rare blank sitting shaker. (No head holes.)

Rare sitting salt and pepper shakers, cold painted in pink and blue.

Rare pink/blue matte finish dresser/grease jar, No. 982 - $800. Unusual paint such as black or yellow bow $800.

Very early cold painted cookie jar and reproduction cookie jar. Notice the reproduction is slightly smaller.

LRRH's basket is the base of a wolf jar. The lid has the flowers and handle. $2000.

Red spray sugar & creamer matches the red spray cookie jar.

LUSTERWARE

Lusterware was manufactured in the late 1920's in beautiful shades of pink, lavender, blue, green and yellow. There are at least thirty-five known molds of vases, jardinieres, etc. in this luster finish.

Row 1

1. flower frog $50
2. low bowl 8" $85
3. bulb bowl 7 1/2" $75
4. bulb bowl 9 1/2" $95
5. console bowl 10" $125

Row 2

1. vase 4" $50
2. vase 6" $75
3. vase 6" $75
4. vase 8" $125
5 & 6. candleholder, each $75

Row 3

1. vase 10" $150
2. vase 10" $125
3. vase 11" $150
4. vase 12" $300
5. vase 13" $250

MAGNOLIA (PINK GLOSS)

This is one of the few glossy patterns produced before the 1950 Hull factory fire. It was made using pink clay and cost more to produce than matte Magnolia pieces. The pink glossy Magnolia was produced in the mid 1950's in shades of pink with darker pink or blue flowers. A few were made in glossy white and trimmed in gold. Gold trimmed pieces usually sell at slightly higher prices.

Row 1

    1. H-1 5 1/2" vase $35

    2. H-2 5 1/2" vase $35

    3. H-3 5 1/2" pitcher...$45

Row 2

    1. H-4 6 1/2" vase $35

    2. H-5 6 1/2" vase $35

    3. H-6 6 1/2" vase $35

    4. H-7 6 1/2" vase $35

Row 3

    1. H-8 8 1/2" vase gold trim..$70

    2. H-9 8 1/2" vase $70

    3. H-10 8 1/2" cornucopia $70

    4. H-11 8 1/2" pitcher(shown in matte finish).................$85

Row 1
1. H-12 10 1/2" vase $85
2. H-13 10 1/2" vase $85
3. H-14 10 1/2" basket...$250
4. H-15 12" double cornucopia..$85

Row 2
1. H-16 12 1/2" winged vase...$200
2. H-17 12 1/2" tassel vase...$200
3. H-18 12 1/2" vase $200
4. H-19 13 1/2" pitcher(shown in matte finish)..............$275

Row 3
1. H-20 6 1/2" teapot gold trimmed............................$165
2. H-21 3 3/4" creamer gold trimmed $50
3. H-22 3 3/4" sugar/lid $50
4. H-23 13" console bowl..$85
5. H-24 4" pair of candleholders $85
6. Copy of Hull pottery vase (poor quality)..................$10

H-15 12" double cornucopia
with experimental point.

Miniature vases with H-12
10 1/2" and H-19 13 1/2"
pitcher.

The Magnolia pattern was produced prolifically in the middle 1940's and was a great favorite. Magnolia pieces are one of the most easily found designs in antique shops due to the many pieces produced. Magnolia is found in shades of brown (from yellow to a dusty rose), and in pink/blue shades.

Row 1

1. 1 8 1/2" vase...$120
2. 2 8 1/2" vase...$115
3. 3 8 1/2" vase...$115
4. 4 6 1/2" vase...$55
5. 5 7" pitcher...$125

Row 2

1. 6 12" double cornucopia $150
2. 7 8 1/2" vase...$115
3. 8 10 1/2" vase...$150
4. 9 10 1/2" vase...$150
5. 10 10 1/2" basket..$300

Row 3

1. 11 6 1/2" vase..$50
2. 12 6 1/2" vase..$55
3. 13 4 3/4" vase..$45
4. 14 4 3/4" pitcher $50
5. 15 6 1/2" vase..$50

MAGNOLIA

Row 1
1. 16 15" floor vase...$425
2. 17 12 1/2" winged vase..$265
3. 18 13 1/2" pitcher $300

Row 2
1. 19 8" cornucopia (hand painted over matte)...............$100
2. 20 15" floor vase...$425
3. 21 12 1/2" tassel vase $275
4. 22 12 1/2" vase...$250

Row 3
1. 23 6 1/2" teapot..$200
2. 24 3 3/4" creamer..$75
3. 25 3 3/4" sugar (no lid) $75
4. 26 12 1/2" console bowl..$150
5. 27 4" candleholders pr. $100

Rare item marked: Hull Art USA
13-4 3/4

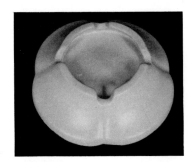

This ashtray was made from the
base of the 20 - 15" vase.

MORNING GLORY

Morning Glory pieces were experimental pieces never put into production. This makes them extremely rare & highly prized to the Hull Collectors Collection.

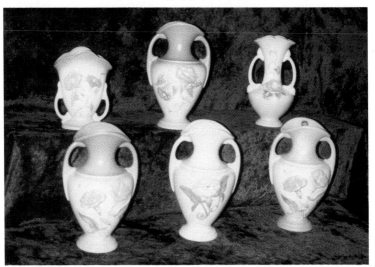

Row 1
1. Vase 6 1/2"...$2000
2. Vase 10 1/2"...$1500
3. Vase 9 1/2"...$2000

Row 2
1. Vase 10 1/2"...$1500
2. Vase (glossy) 10 1/2"...$1000
3. Vase 10 1/2"...$1500

MINIATURES

Miniatures in pastel glazes and white were introduced to the Hull line in 1940.

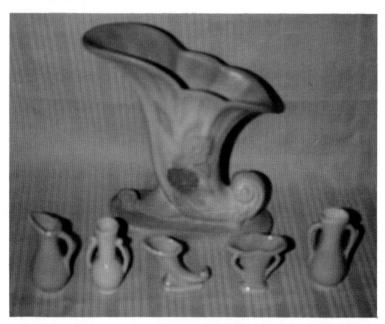

Pitcher A, white vase (lettering unreadable), cornucopia F, fan vase C, vase D. These miniatures are owned by Bryon & Gerald Donaldson.

← Note Hull label on miniature vase.

These → miniatures of Hull are owned by Duke Frash.

These miniatures were photographed in the Higginbotham collection.

The oven proof Nuline Bak-Serve kitchenware pieces appeared in the late 1930's in shades of rose, light peach, and blues. The designs were marked by a B for a diamond effect, a C for scales, and a D for a paneled effect. The molds were for bowls, bean pots, pitchers, casseroles and other kitchen items.

Row 1

   1. B-6 6 1/2" bowl $25

   2. B-6 8 1/2" bowl $35

   3. B-13 7 1/2" casserole with lid $50

Row 2

   1. B-20 cookie jar (no lid)..$50

   2. B-29 pitcher $85

OLD SPICE

Hull manufactured Old Spice mugs for the use of the Shulton Company in the 1930's and 1940's. The glazed mug features the picture of a blue sailing ship with Old Spice written in Red.

Old Spice Mug ....$20-$40

OPEN ROSE/CAMELLIA

The Open Rose or Camellia pattern is one of the most prolific in the Hull matte finish patterns. The Open Rose or Camellia design on pink/cream/blue, white, or cream background is truly a beautiful pattern.

Row 1

1. 101 8 1/2" cornucopia $130
2. 102 8 1/2" vase..$140
3. 103 8 1/2" vase..$155
4. 104 10 1/2" mermaid planter.....................$3500-$5000
5. 105 7" pitcher..$225

Row 2

1. 106 13 1/2" pitcher $575
2. 107 6" basket..$350
3. 108 8 1/2" vase..$200
   109 10 1/2" vase..Rare
4. 110 8 1/2" teapot..$350
5. 111 5" creamer..$85
6. 112 5" sugar $85

Row 3

1. 113 7" bowl....................................$125
2. 114 8 1/2" jardiniere with
   rams head handles...........................$375
3. 115 8 1/2" pitcher............................$300
4. 116 12" console bowl........................$300
5-6. 117 6 1/2" dove candle-
   holders pr...$295

No. 109 10 1/2"
vase - rare.

* The 104 mermaid has been reproduced. Watch carefully to make sure the base measures a full 10 1/2".

Row 1

1. 118 6 1/2" swan vase..$135
2. 119 8 1/2" vase...$175
3. 120 6 1/4" vase...$110
4. 121 6 1/4" vase...$110

Row 2

1. 122 6 1/4" vase...$110
2. 123 6 1/2" vase...$115
3. 124 12" vase $350
4. 125 8 1/2" wall pocket $325

Row 3

1. 126 8 1/2" hand vase...$300
2. 127 4 3/4" vase...$75
3. 128 4 3/4" pitcher $85
4. 129 7" bud vase..$145

Row 1

1. 130 4 3/4" vase...$75
2. 131 4 3/4" vase...$85
3. 132 7" hanging basket $250
4. 133 6 1/4" vase...$130
5. 134 6 1/4" vase...$140

Row 2

1. 135 6 1/4" vase...$135
2. 136 6 1/4" vase...$135
3. 137 6 1/4" vase...$135
4. 138 6 1/4" vase...$140

Row 3

1. 139 10 1/2" lamp vase...................................$475
2. 140 10 1/2" basket.......................................$1300
3. 141 8 1/2" cornucopia $150
4. 142 6 1/4" basket..$325
5. 143 8 1/2" vase...$195

Orchid, a lovely matte finish pottery manufactured in the late 1930's, was produced in more than one size in many of the molds. Colors are shades of pink/blue, cream/blue, and pink/cream.

Row 1

NP. 300 6 1/2" vase $135
1. 301 4 3/4" vase..$95
2. 301 6" vase $140
3. 301 8 1/2" vase..$185
4. 301 10" vase $325

Row 2

1. 302 4 3/4" vase..$95
2. 302 6" vase $145
3. 302 8" vase $195
4. 302 10" vase $325

Row 3

1. 303 4 3/4" vase..$95
2. 303 6" vase $140
3. 303 8" vase $195
4. 303 10" vase $325
NP. 304 4 1/2" vase $95
5. 304 6" vase $140
6. 304 8 1/2" vase..$195
7. 304 10 1/4" vase...$325

Row 1

1. 305 7" basket $525
2. 306 6 3/4" bud base $145
3. 307 4 3/4" vase $100
4. 307 6 1/2" vase $145
NP. 307 8" vase $195
NP. 307 10" vase $325
5. 308 4 3/4" vase $95
6. 308 6 1/2" vase $145
NP. 308 8" vase $195
NP. 308 10" vase $325
7. 309 8 1/2" vase $195

Row 2

1. 310 4 3/4" jardiniere $120
2. 310 6" jardiniere $225
3. 310 9 1/2" jardiniere $425
4. 311 13" pitcher $650
5. 312 7" bowl $135

Row 3

1. 314 13" console bowl $325
2. 315 4" candleholders pr. $225
3 & 4. 316 7" bookends $1200
5. 317 4 3/4" jardiniere $95

Pine sprays make up the design for the Parchment & Pine pottery manufactured in the early 1950's in high gloss shades of green and brown.

Row 1
1. S-1 5" vase $50
2. S-2 R 8" cornucopia $50
3. S-2 L 8" cornucopia...$50
4. S-3 6" basket...$75
5. S-4 10" vase $75
6. S-5 10 1/2" window box $85

Row 2
1. S-6 L 12" cornucopia..$90
2. S-6 R 12" cornucopia $90
3. S-7 13 1/2" pitcher $185
4. S-8 16" basket..$160
5. S-9 16" console bowl...$95

Row 3
1. S-10 2 1/4" candleholders pr.......................................$50
2. S-11 6" teapot...$100
3. S-12 3 1/4" creamer $35
4. S-13 3 1/4" sugar with lid..$35
5. S-14 14" ash tray...$110
6. S-15 8" coffee pot..$125

PAGODA

Twelve molds were used in manufacturing the Pagoda pattern in 1960. They include vases & planters in shades of orange, green & white. Prices range from $10 to $40.

PINE CONE

The very beautiful Pine Cone pattern was manufactured in the late 1930's in only one mold, however it does come in several shades of pinks, blues, and turquoise. $150.

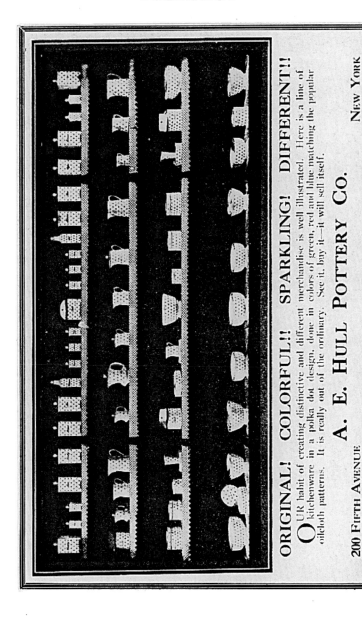

POPPY

Poppy flowers decorate this mold manufactured in the 1940's in lovely shades of pink/blue, cream and pink/cream. This pattern features more than one size in several of the molds.

Row 1

1. 601 9" basket $750
2. 601 12" basket $1300
3. 602 6 1/2" planter $295

Row 2

1. 603 4 3/4" jardiniere $175
2. 604 8" cornucopia $325
NP. 605 4 3/4" vase $175
NP. 605 6 1/2" vase $195
3. 605 8 1/2" vase $250
NP. 605 10 1/2" vase $450
NP. 606 4 3/8" vase $175
4. 606 6 1/2" vase $200
5. 606 8 1/2" vase $250
6. 606 10 1/2" vase $425

Row 3

1. 607 4 3/4" vase $175
2. 607 6 1/2" vase $195
3. 607 8 1/2" vase $250
4. 607 10 1/2" vase $425

Row 1
1. 608 4 3/4" jardiniere ...$150
2. 609 9" wall planter $450

Row 2
1. 610 4 3/4" pitcher $200
2. 610 13" pitcher $850
NP. 611 4 3/4" vase.........$175

3. 611 6 1/2" vase.............$200
NP. 611 8 1/2" vase.........$250
NP. 611 10 1/2" vase.......$450
NP. 612 4 3/4" vase.........$175
4. 612 6 1/2" vase.............$200
NP. 612 8" vase $250
NP. 612 10 1/2" vase.......$400

PAINT TUMBLERS

These 3 1/2" tumblers were used to experiment on paint colors and finishes before putting new designs into production. - $10.

ROSELLA

Rosella is one of the few high gloss Hull patterns manufactured before 1950. It was manufactured in the late 1940's in shades of pink and ivory.

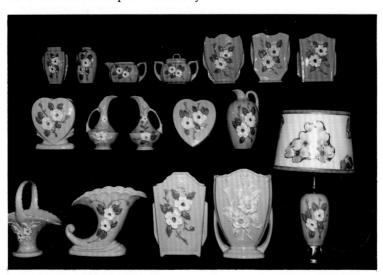

Row 1

1. R-1 5" vase \$35
2. R-2 5" vase \$35
3. R-3 5 1/2" creamer...\$50
4. R-4 5 1/2" sugar/lid...\$60
5. R-5 6 1/2" vase...\$45
6. R-6 6 1/2" vase...\$45
7. R-7 6 1/2" vase...\$45

Row 2

1. R-8 6 1/2" vase...\$75
2. R-9 6 1/2" L pitcher..\$75
3. R-9 6 1/2" R pitcher..\$75
4. R-10 6 1/2" hanging planter.......................................\$85
5. R-11 7" R pitcher \$85

Row 3

1. R-12 7" basket..\$185
2. R-13 8 1/2" L cornucopia..\$75
3. R-14 8 1/2" vase...\$75
4. R-15 8 1/2" vase...\$75
5. 6 3/4" lamp...\$300

The Royal pottery was made in the 1950's after the factory fire. It is in high gloss pink or turquoise with a spattered effect and black shading. Woodland, Ebb Tide, Imperial, and other mold shapes were used in the manufacturing of many Royal pieces. There are many more pieces than are pictured here.

Row 1

1. E1 6 1/2" Ebb Tide fish vase $35
2. W4 6 1/2" Woodland vase $35
3. W6 6 1/2" Woodland pitcher.......................................$45
4. W8 7 1/2" Woodland vase $40
5. W9 8 3/4" Woodland basket..$50
6. W10 11" Woodland Cornucopia................................$45

Row 2

1. W13 7 1/2" Woodland shell wall planter.................$50
2. W22 10 1/2" Woodland basket..............................$135
3. W26 Woodland teapot $95
4. W28 Woodland creamer $25
5. W29 13" Woodland console bowl $75
6. W30 Woodland candleholder $25

Row 3

1. 65 6" pedestal planter...$25
2. 75 6" jardiniere $35
3-4. 86 & 87 Butterfly lavo bowl set...........................$100
5. 91 pigeon planter $30
6. 93 love birds..$30

The green dino bank was an advertising special for Sinclair. The rare advertising sign is green also.

The Little Texan Bank was made for Graham Chevrolet of Mansfield, Ohio in 1972 as a promotional item for Mr. Graham's car dealership. These banks were hand-painted by Gladys Showers in her home. Gladys is the widow of Harold Showers who was the plant manager of the Hull Pottery Company more than 40 years. She was the plant's nurse for over 10 years. The bank reads "The Little Texan Save at Graham Chevytown, Mansfield, Ohio".

This Marilyn Monroe planter is the only one made by Louise Bauer.

This 16" reclining Indian is displayed at the Ohio ceramic center. Designed for a client in the late 1930's, it proved too expensive and was not put into production.

The Star Flower vase came from the mold room after the flood and fire at the Hull Pottery Company in 1950. Loads of pottery were hauled to the dump. This vase was later rescued from the dump.

SERENADE

The Serenade pattern featuring beautiful birds was manufactured in the late 1950's. Serenade pieces come in shades of light yellow, blue and pink. Serenade has become one of the fastest selling of the Post 1950 patterns.

Row 1
1. S1 6" vase...$50
2. S2 6" pitcher..$60
3. S3 5 3/4" pedestal planter................................$50
4. S3C 8 1/4" candy dish with lid.......................$95
5. S4 5" hat shaped vase.......................................$55
6. S5 6 3/4" basket...$95

Row 2
1. S6 8 1/2" vase...$55
2. S7 8 1/2" vase...$55
3. S8 8 1/2" pitcher...$85
4. S9 12 1/2" window box.....................................$95
5. S10 11" cornucopia...$95
6. S11 10 1/2" vase...$95

Row 3
1. S12 14" vase...........................$125
2. S13 13 1/2" pitcher..................$375
3. S14 12" basket.........................$350
4. S15 11 1/2" footed fruit bowl..$110
5. S16 6 1/2" candleholders pr......$70

Row 4
1. S17 6 cup teapot.......................$175
2. S18 3 1/2" creamer....................$45
3. S19 3 1/2" sugar with lid..........$45
4. S20 9" covered casserole...........$125
5. S21 1 1/2 qt. pitcher.................$125
6. S22 8 oz. mug............................$55
7. S 23 13x10 1/2" ash tray.............$95

Beautiful S-14 basket heavily trimmed in gold.

STONEWARE

The Stoneware pieces of Hull manufactured in the 1920's came in a multitude of colors, molds, sizes and shapes in both the matte and gloss finish. These pieces are marked with an H enclosed in a circle or a diamond. See Page 6, No.1.

Row 1
1. 25 ⊕ vase 5 1/2" $65
2. 26 ⊕ vase 8" $80
3. 32 ⊕ vase 8" $80
4. 32 ⊕ vase 8" $80
5. 40 ⊕ vase 7" $95
6. 39 ⊕ vase 8" $80

Row 2
1. 536 ⊕ jardiniere 5" $65
2. 536 ⊕ jardiniere 8" $95
3. 536 ⊕ jardiniere 9" $110
4. 546 ⊕ jardiniere 3" $65
5. 546 ⊕ jardiniere 4" $65
6. 546 ⊕ jardiniere 7" $90

Row 3
1. 550 ⊕ jardiniere 7" $90
2. 551 ⊕ jardiniere 7" $90
3. Vase, unmarked 7"..$75
4. Hanging basket, unmarked 5" $100
5. Hanging basket, unmarked 5" $100
6. Flower pot with saucer, unmarked 6" $70

Row 1
1. ⊕ jardiniere 5 1/2" $150
2. ⊕ vase 4 1/2"..$60
3. ⊕ vase 4 1/2"..$60
4. ⊕ vase 4 1/2"..$60
5. ⊕ jardiniere 5 1/4" $135

Row 2
1. ⊕ flower pot 6"..$60
2. ⊕ flower pot 6"..$60
3. ⊕ flower pot 6"..$60

Row 3
1. ⊕ bowl 3" $85
2. ⊕ flower pot 4"..$40
3. ⊕ flower pot 3 3/4" $35
4. ⊕ flower pot 4"..$40
5. ⊕ vase 5 1/2"..$65

Row 1

1. 492 ⊕ stein 6 1/2"...$45
2. 495 ⊕ flying Order of the Eagles stein........................$75
3. 492 ⊕ covered pretzel jar 9 1/2"...............................$275
4. 492 ⊕ tankard...$150
5. 496 ⊕ Elk stein 6 1/2"..$75
6. American Legion stein 6 1/2".....................................$75

Row 2

1. 491 ⊕ mug 4 3/4"...$45
2. 493 ⊕ mug 4 1/4"...$45
3. 493 ⊕ mug 4 1/4"...$45
4. 494 ⊕ mug 4 1/2"...$45
5. 497 ⊕ "Happy Days Are Here Again" mug 4 3/4".$45
6. 497 ⊕ "Happy Days Are Here Again" mug 4 3/4".$45

Some harder to find Stoneware pieces are the flowered ⊕ 6", $95; Tassel 4 3/4", $50 and the Ivy 7 1/2", $95, planters.

Rare handled vase, unmarked 6 1/2" - $95.

Row 1

1. ◈ coffee canister 6 1/2" $100
2. ◈ sugar canister 6 1/2"..$100
3. ◈ tea canister 6 1/2"..$100
4. ◈ rice canister 6 1/2" $100

Row 2

1. ◈ semi-porcelain pitcher 4 1/4" $80
2. ◈ spice jar 3 1/2" $80
3. ◈ pepper jar 3 1/2" $80
4. ◈ nutmeg jar 3 1/2" $80
5. ◈ mustard jar 3 1/2" $80
6. ◈ spice jar 3 1/2" $80
7. ◈ ginger jar 3 1/2"...$80
8. ◈ spice jar 3 1/2" $80
9. ◈ semi-porcelain pitcher 6 3/4" $100

Row 3

1. vase 6" $65
2. 421 bowl 5" $30
3. 160 custard 2 1/2"...$20
4. bowl 10 1/2" $85
5. 421 bowl 5" $30
6. bean pot with lid 5" $85

STONEWARE

Row 1

1. 100 ⊕ covered bowl 5 1/2"...$75
2. 100 ⊕ bowl 4"..$30
3. 100 ⊕ bowl 5"...$35
4. 100 ⊕ bowl 7"...$45
5. 100 ⊕ bowl 8"...$55
6. 100 ⊕ bowl 9"...$65
7. 100 ⊕ bowl 12"...$85

Row 2

1. 106 ⊕ handled bake dish 4"...$40
2. 106 ⊕ bake dish 4"..$30
3. 106 ⊕ bake dish 6"...$40
4. 106 ⊕ bake dish 8"...$50
5. 106 ⊕ bake dish 9"...$55

Row 3

1. 106 ⊕ pitcher...................................$60
2. 106 ⊕ pitcher...................................$70
3. 111 ⊕ salt box 6".........................$130
4. 114 ⊕ custard cup 2"....................$25
5. 114 ⊕ custard cup 2".....................$25
6. 113 ⊕ covered casserole 7 1/2" ...$75

RARE Stone jar found in Minnesota.

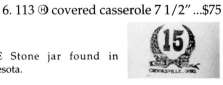

Sun Glow pottery is a glossy pink or yellow pansy and butterfly design manufactured in the early 1950's for ten cent store distribution.

Row 1
1. Bell $150
2. Bell (Loop or
      Needle Handle)....$175
3. 83 Iron Wall Pocket $65
4. 50-5 1/2" Bowl $20
5. 50 -7 1/2" Bowl $30
6. 50-9 1/2" Bowl $40
7. 51-7 1/2" Covered
      Casserole $50

Row 2
1. 52 24 oz. Pitcher $35
2. 53 Grease Jar $35
3. 54 Salt & Pepper
         Shakers $20
4. 55 7 1/2" Beverage
         Pitcher $85
5. 80 Cup / Saucer /
         Wall Pocket.............$65
6. 81 Pitcher / Wall
         Pocket $65

7. 82 Whisk Broom/
         Wall Pocket.............$65

Row 3
1. 84 6 1/2" Basket $65
2. 85 8 3/4" Bird Vase $45
3. 88 5 1/2" Vase $35
4. 89 5 1/2" Vase $35
5. 90 5 1/2" Pitcher $40
6. 91 6 1/2" Vase $40
7. 92 6 1/2" Vase $40
8. 93 6 1/2" Vase $40

Row 4
1. 94 8" Vase....................$45
2. 95 8 1/2" Vase $45
3. 96 8 1/2" Cornucopia.$50
4. 97 5 1/2" Flower Pot ..$35
5. 98 7 1/2" Flower Pot ..$45
6. 99 6" Hanging Basket.$65
7. 100 6 1/2" Vase $40

SUPREME

Made in 1960 these Supreme items are considered experimental as they were never sold on the market. Colors are shades of green and brown & orange.

Row 1
     1. urn 6" $100
     2. urn 4 1/2" $100
     3. bowl 4 1/4" $100

Row 2
     1. candy dish 7" $125
     2. basket 8 1/2" $125
     3. vase 8" $75

Row 3
     1. vase 12 1/2" $175
     2. pitcher 10" $200
     3. pedestal vase 10" $150
     4. lamp 12 1/2" $200

Only four molds were used to make the Thistle pattern in the late 1930's in colors of pink, blue, or turquoise. Numbered 51, 52, 53, 54, all are 6 1/2" - $125-$150.

TILE

Wall and floor tiles were manufactured by Hull in the late 1920's and into the 1930's in a large variety of colors in both matte and gloss finishes. The tiles are 4 1/4" x 4 1/4". The border tile is 2 7/8" x 6". Most of the tiles pictured were purchased in Crooksville, Ohio. They range in price from $25-$300. The tile marked "Pottery Lover's Reunion 1985" was a souvenir gift at that festival.

Back side of tile marked:
Hull - CUSHION TILE.

These nine-tiles are deep black/brown with gold in three dimensional patterns.

Martha & George Washington tiles found in a garage in Crooksville.

The blue and white ship and the pink and blue Fleur-de-lis tiles are marked Hull Faience.

    This window grouping of over 100 tiles was used on the wall behind a soda fountain in a Milwaukee drugstore until 1950 and has been in storage since. The tiles are marked HULL Faience. Faience tiles usually have unglazed edges for cement and grout installation.

    The colors in these tiles are beautiful. The tiles on the border are brown/black showing lots of gold. The tiny border tiles with a rolling pin design and the tiles with designs are three dimensional and created by the squeeze-bag process. This grouping is extremely beautiful and a rare find.

Tokay/Tuscany is a high gloss pottery with grape and leaf designs. It was manufactured in the late 1950's in white/dark green and shades of green/pink.

Row 1
1. 1 6 1/2" cornucopia...........................$40
2. 2 6" vase...$40
3. 3 8" pitcher $95
4. 4 8 1/4" vase......................................$90
5. 5 5 1/2" jardiniere $55
6. 6 8" basket...$95
7. 7 9 1/2" fruit bowl...........................$150
8. 8 10" vase...$125

Row 2
1. 9 compote..$65
2. 9C 8 1/2" candy dish $100
3. 10 11" cornucopia $65
4. 11 10 1/2" moon basket...................$125
5. 12 12" vase..$110
6. 13 12" pitcher $200

Row 3
1. 14 15 3/4" con-
          solette $165
2. 15 12" basket..............$200
3. 16 teapot......................$150
4. 17 creamer.....................$50
5. 18 sugar with lid $50
6. 19 leaf dish $95
7. 21 14" pitcher $225

This hard to find Tokay number 20 is 15" tall - $225.

These beautifully colored Tokay & Blossomflite pieces were photographed in Louise Bauer's private studio.

TROPICANA

There are only seven known, highly sought after Tropicana molds. Made in the late 1950's, Tropicana is a glossy white featuring Caribbean people.

Row 1
1. T51 5 1/2" flower dish $425
2. T52 10"x 7 1/2" ashtray..$425
3. T53 8 1/2" vase $450

Row 2
1. T54 12 1/2" vase $500
2. T55 12 3/4" basket...........$700
3. T56 13 1/2" pitcher..........$750
4. T57 14 1/2" hanging
     planter vase......................$600

The three experimental T53 vases are from the Higginbotham collection.

This Tropicana basket has a rough texture and is painted yellow much like the Serenade pieces. This possible "one-of-a-kind" basket is owned by Steve Johnson.

The Tulip design vases appeared in the late thirties in shades of pink/blue and cream/blue. Some molds are offered in a variety of sizes.

Row 1

1. 100-33-4" vase...$85
2. 100-33-6 1/2" vase $125
3. 100-33-8" vase...$185
4. 100-33-10" vase..$295

Row 2

NP. 101-33-6 1/2" vase..$125
1. 101-33-9" vase...$245
NP. 101-33-10" vase $350
2. 102-33-6" basket $250
3. 103-33-6" suspended vase...$250

Row 3

1. 104-44-6" bud vase...$125
2. 105-33-8" vase...$225
3. 106-33-6 1/2" vase $125
4. 107-33-6" vase...$125
NP. 107-33-8" vase $200
107-33-8" lamp (see Page 56) $600
107-33-10" lamp (see Page 56) $700

Row 1

   1. 108-33-6" vase $125
   2. 109-33-8" pitcher $235
   3. 109-33-13' pitcher $400

Row 2

   1. 110-33-6" vase $150
   2. 111-33-6" vase $150
   3. 115-33-7" large jardiniere $325

Row 3

   1. 116-33-4 3/4" flower pot with attached saucer $125
   NP. 116-33-6" flower pot with attached saucer $195
   2. 117-30-5" jardiniere $125
   4. lamp (same mold as 115-7") $600

Water Lily was manufactured in the late 1940's with the water lily flower on water markings. Water Lily is found in shades of tan/brown or pink/turquoise. A few pieces were manufactured in a glossy white with gold trim. Items trimmed in gold are usually slightly higher in price.

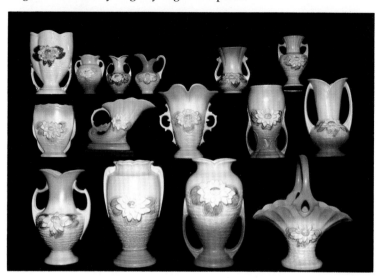

Row 1
1. L-A-8 1/2" vase..$170
2. L-1-5 1/2" vase..$55
3. L-2-5 1/2" vase..$55
4. L-3-5 1/2" pitcher $95
5. L-4-6 1/2" vase..$90
6. L-5-6 1/2" vase..$85

Row 2
1. L-6-6 1/2" vase $95
2. L-7-6 1/2" cornucopia $80
3. L-8-8 1/2" vase $145
4. L-9-8 1/2" vase $175
5. L-10-9 1/2" vase $175

Row 3
1. L-11-9 1/2" vase $175
2. L-12-10 1/2" vase $200
3. L-13-10 1/2" vase $200
4. L-14-10 1/2" basket...................$350

Water Lily's L-17 13 1/2" pitcher painted in yellow with a pink flower.

This L-18-6" teapot has a rare ivory & apple green matte finish.

Row 1
   1. L-15-12 1/2" vase..$395
   2. L-16-12 1/2" vase..$395
   3. L-17-12 1/2" pitcher $425
Row 2
   1. L-18-6" teapot...$225
   2. L-19-5" creamer...$75
   3. L-20-5" sugar with lid $75
   4. L-21-13 1/2" console bowl..$175
   5. L-22-4" candleholders pr. $125
Row 3
   1. L-23-5 1/2" jardiniere...$125
   2. L-24-8 1/2" large jardiniere...$325
   3. L-25-5 1/4" planter with attached saucer.................$165
   4. L-27-12" double cornucopia $225

One of Hull's most popular designs is the Wildflower pattern featuring the three petaled Trillium flower making it easy to identify. It was manufactured in the 1940's, beginning with the numbered series from 51 to 79. The later series is numbered with a W from 1 to 21. Colors are in shades of tan/brown and pink/blue.

Row 1
1. W-1-5 1/2" vase $55
2. W-2-5 1/2" pitcher..$85
3. W-3-5 1/2" vase $55
4. W-4-6 1/2" vase $80
5. W-5-6 1/2" vase $80

Row 2
1. W-6-7 1/2" vase $90
2. W-7-7 1/2" cornucopia $85
3. W-8-7 1/2" vase $85
4. W-9-8 1/2" vase $145
5. W-10-8 1/2" cornucopia $100

Row 3
1. W-11-8 1/2" pitcher..$165
2. W-12-9 1/2" vase $155
3. W-13-9 1/2" vase $155
4. W-14-10 1/2" vase $175

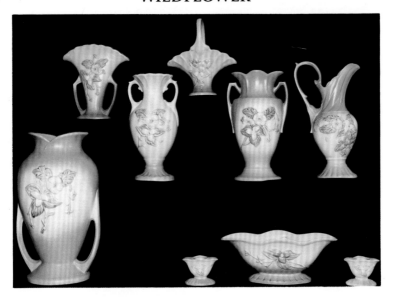

Row 1

1. W-15-10 1/2" fan vase...$175
2. W-16-10 1/2" basket (solid handle) $375
NP. W-16-10 1/2" basket (hole in handle)..........................$375

Row 2

1. W-17-12 1/4" vase $250
2. W-18-12 1/2" vase $250
3. W-19-13 1/2" pitcher...$450

Row 3

1. W-20-15" floor vase $475
2. W-21-12" console bowl..$145
3. candleholders pr. $120

This W-15-10 1/2" vase has a rare pebble finish. Photographed in Louise Bauer's studio.

A lucky buyer found this W-23 tea pot at an auction in Ohio in 1994. Where is the sugar & creamer?

Row 1
1. 51 8 1/2" vase $295
2. 52 5 1/2" vase $155
3. 53 8 1/2" vase $295
4. 54 6 1/2" vase $145

Row 2
1. 55 13 1/2" pitcher $1200
2. 56 4 1/2" vase $120
3. 57 4 1/2" pitcher $145
4. 58 6 1/2" cornucopia $145
5. 59 10 1/2" vase $325

Row 3
1. 60 6 1/2" vase $170
2. 61 6 1/2" vase $160
3. 62 6 1/2" vase $160
4. 63 7 1/2" pitcher $350
5. 64 4" jardiniere $125
6. 65 7" low basket $795

WILD FLOWER

Row 1

1. 64 4" jardiniere $125
2. 65 7" low basket $795
3. 66 10 1/4" basket...$2000
4. 67 8 1/2" vase $325
5. 68 7 1/2" cornucopia $135

Row 2

1 & 3. 69 4" candleholders pr. $250
2. 70 12" console bowl $350
4. 71 12" vase $395
5. 72 8" teapot $1200
6. 73 4 3/4" creamer...$250
7. 74 4 3/4" sugar $250

Row 3

1. 75 8 1/2" vase.............$325
2. 76 8 1/2" vase.............$325
3. 77 10 1/2" vase...........$395
4. 78 8 1/2" vase.............$325
5. 79 10 1/4" basket $2000

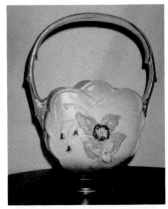

Some Hull Pottery was sold to other companies who painted and sold them under their own company's sticker. These Wild Flower items are gold and brown with bright orange and blue flowers.

The Woodland pieces were manufactured in three different finishes during the late 1940's and early 1950's. The oldest molds feature a yellow center in the flower and come in shades of cream, rose and green. Those manufactured after the 1950 factory fire in the matte finish are not as durable as the earlier pieces. These items come in rose, yellow and green. The newest molds were painted a very high gloss in two-tone shades featuring chartreuse, dark green, blue, rose and white.

	Pre 1950	Post 1950	Glossy
Row 1			
1. W1 5 1/2" vase	$95		$40
2. W2 5 1/2" cornucopia	$95	$85	$40
3. W3 5 1/2" pitcher	$125	$75	$45
4. W4 6 1/2" vase	$125	$100	$45
Page 120 W5 6 1/2" cornucopia	$75		
5. W6 6 1/4" pitcher	$110	$100	$65
Row 2			
1. W7 5 1/4" jardiniere	$140	$125	$65
2. W8 7 1/4" vase	$125	$125	$60
3. W9 8 3/4" basket	$245	$175	$110
4. W10 11" cornucopia (shown in glossy white with gold trim)	$195	$95	$65
5. W11 5 1/2" flower pot with attached saucer	$165	$135	$75
Row 3			
1. W12 7 1/2" hanging basket	$550		
2. W13 7 1/2" shell wall pocket	$165	$145	$95
3. W14 10" window box	$145	$150	$65
4. W15 8 1/2" double vase	$145	$165	$65
5. W16 8 1/2" vase	$185	$155	$80

WOODLAND

Row 1	Pre 1950	Post 1950	Glossy
1. W17 7 1/2" suspended vase	$250		
2. W18 10 1/2" vase	$175	$125	$95
3. W19 10 1/2" window box	$135		$95
4. W21 9 1/2" jardiniere	$650	$500	$275
Row 2			
1. W22 10 1/2" basket	$750	$400	$250
2. W23 14" double cornucopia	$475		
3. W24 13 1/2" pitcher	$575	$275	$225
4. W25 12 1/2" vase	$395		
Row 3			
1. W26 6 1/2" teapot	$350	$175	$125
2. W27 4 1/2" creamer	$75	$50	$35
3. W28 3 1/2" sugar with lid	$75	$50	$35
4. W29 14" console bowl	$295	$175	$100
5. W30 3 1/2" candleholder ea.	$65	$50	$35
6. W31 5 1/2" hanging basket	$145		

A few pieces of Woodland were manufactured in high gloss white and trimmed in gold. Because of the gold trim, these pieces usually command a slightly higher price than the regular matte molds.

Produced in the late 1920's, Zane Grey is a blue banded white kitchen ware product. The molds include mixing bowls, pitcher, covered jar, jugs, and other items. The covered jars sell for as high as $300, bowls from $20 to $75, jugs from $25 to $100, and other items selling at similar prices of $10 to $100 and up.

HULL NEWSLETTER EDITORS

Kim & Dan Pfaff are the Editors of the Hull Newsletter ($22 a year). You can have a free ad each month to buy or sell Hull items. (466 Foreston Place, Webster Groves, MO. 63119) 314-963-1087.

HAND PAINTED DINNERWARE

Nancy and Al Dennis were managers of the Ohio Ceramic Center (pottery museum) for six years. In 1986 when the Hull factory closed the greenware left in the plant was given to the Ohio Ceramic Center. Nancy hand painted the greenware and it was sold at the Ohio Ceramic Center to the lucky collectors who visited the museum. The Dennis' have retired and the supply of hand painted items has been sold.

By Dee Konyha

The A.E. Hull Pottery Company was founded in 1905 by Addis Emmet Hull, William Watts, and J.D. Young in Crooksville, Ohio. The Company's production focused on stoneware. In 1907 the Acme Pottery Company, a producer of semi-porcelain dinnerware, was purchased by a brother, an incorporator of the company who also served as President of the Board of Directors.

After World War I, the company manufactured toilet, kitchen, and lusterware in addition to a line of stoneware items. From 1921 to the Stock Market Crash of 1929, earthenware china and pottery items from Europe were also imported by the Hull company and sold as imported items for less than their own production costs. In 1927 one plant was converted to tiling operations. Three types of tiles were produced: matte, gloss or stipled finishes. Accessory items were also available in matching colors. By 1933 the price of tiles were less than the production costs, and they were discontinued.

When Addis E. Hull, Sr., died in 1930, the oldest son, Addis E. Hull, Jr., took over the company and production continued to consist of lines of stoneware, kitchenware, gardenware, and floristware. In 1937 A.E. Hull, Jr., left the company to manage the Shawnee Pottery Company of Zanesville, Ohio. Gerald F. Watts, son of William Watts, became President of the company. Also in 1937, the company contracted with Shulton of New York for the manufacture of shaving mugs, after shave lotion, cologne and after shave talc bottles. This production continued until 1944. In the late 30's (1938), the first art pottery lines were introduced, which included the Tulip, Calla Lily, Thistle, Pinecone, and Orchid patterns.

During the forties, the matte art pottery lines flourished at the A.E. Hull Pottery Company. These art lines included Iris, Dogwood, Poppy, Open Rose, Magnolia, Wildflower, Wild Flower (Number Series), Water Lily, Granada/Mardi Gras, Bow Knot, and Woodland. Many of these pieces have the marks of the decorator on the bottom. Each decorator had a number and/or letter. Two high gloss lines were also produced during this time - Rosella and Magnolia. Rosella was only offered during 1946 because of high costs involved in producing the pink base clay at the factory.

In addition to the art pottery being produced at this time, kitchenware items continued, plus novelty items were introduced in the early 1940's. The year 1943 was highlighted by the introduction of the Red Riding Hood cookie jar, which was patented June 29, 1943 by Louise E. Bauer of Zenesville, Ohio. She assigned her rights to the patent design to the A.E. Hull Company, Inc., of Crooksville, Ohio. "Little Red Riding Hood" items were soon in great demand - and still are today. However, the A.E. Hull Company did not trim or decorate these items. Blanks produced by Hull were sent to the Royal China and Novelty Company of Chicago, Illinois, who decorated the items.

Disaster struck on June 16, 1950, when a flood and subsequent fire destroyed the plant, equipment, and office records; including formulas, mold designs, payroll, accounts, etc. Under the direction of J.B. Hull, on January 1, 1952, a new plant opened with the name changed to The Hull Pottery Company.

Art lines were again produced with Louise Bauer as designer. Woodland, which has been introduced prior to the disaster, was again produced but proved that the pre-1950 matte finish could not be duplicated. It was then manufactured in two tone and white high gloss colors. Subsequent art lines which were unique to themselves included: Parchment and Pine, Sunglow, Ebb Tide, Classic, Blossom Flite, Butterfly, Serenade, Royal Woodland, Fiesta, Tokay, Tropicana, and Continental. Vast numbers of novelty items including swans, banks, dogs, cats, and a wide variety of kitchenware items were also produced during the fifties.

The sixties demonstrated a production change from art lines (Tuscany) to predominately House 'n Garden serving ware and Imperial florist ware which continued through the seventies. Initially, House 'n Garden serving ware was produced in the high gloss color of Mirror Brown, but later in Tangerine, Green, Agate, and Butterscotch. This combination was called Rainbow, and advertised as such in assorted colors. Crestone was another casual serving ware produced in a high gloss turquoise with white foam edge color.

In 1978 J. B. Hull died, and Henry Sulens became President, with Robert W. Hull as Chairman of the Board of Directors. In 1981 Larry Taylor replaced Sulens as the President until the factory closed in March, 1986. In the closing years, the company was plagued with multiple union strikes and competition from foreign made wares which were cheaper to produce and market. During those years, until 1985, the company continued to make dinnerware lines which included the House 'n Garden Line, the Ridge Collection, Heartland, and Blue Belle.

The Hull factory closed its doors in 1986. The building was sold to the Friendship Pottery Company and as they were remodeling the building it caught fire in August of 1993 and burned to the ground closing again another chapter of Hull history.

Louise Bauer and Stanley Martens outside the studio where Louise designed Hull pottery from 1949 to 1985.

The Friendship Pottery Company had removed the Hull pottery sign and put up the new sign in preparation in opening the plant.

In August of 1993 the plant burned to the ground before it was officially open for business.

Joe Yonis displayed some of the many pieces of pottery at the 1994 Hull Convention that were uncovered under the foundation of the Hull plant after the fire.

Many designs believed to be Hull were confirmed by finding pieces of pottery under the factory.

THE AUTHOR

Joan Gray Hull was born in Oklahoma, and moved to South Dakota when she married Vernon W. Hull. She has a master's degree in Guidance and Counseling from South Dakota State University, and was high school counselor for 20 years. She opted for early retirement to write **HULL The Heavenly Pottery**, and to pursue other interests in writing and working as a travel guide.

She has received numerous awards including: National Solo parent Mother of the Year, National Solo Parent President, South Dakota Counselor of the Year, and was the 1985 South Dakota Mother of the Year.

Widowed at an early age, she raised four daughters. When asked about her children, she usually quips, "They are all grown, educated, happily married, gainfully employed, and they don't call home collect". The daughters have presented Joan with eight grandchildren (so far): Erikka, Erinn, Jill, Jon, Jade, Cole, Will, and Sydney Cathlene.

Mrs. Hull does a great deal of public speaking and travelogues both in and out of South Dakota. Joan writes a weekly humor column for the Huron Plainsman. She has co-authored a book with her brother, Robert Gray, **Shades of Gray**, has had articles published in the Antique Trader and The Glaze, and is the Hull price expert in **Warman's Antiques** and **Warman's Americana and Collectibles.**

BIBLIOGRAPHY

Bauer, Louise. Personal interviews 1985,1989, 1992, 1993 & 1994

Burke, Barbara. **Hull Pottery The Dinnerware Lines**

Burks, John H. Personal correspondence.

Hull, Byron. Hull Pottery plant, July 1985.

Hull, Joan. **The Antique Trader Weekly:** Hull Pottery - The End and The Beginning. January 13, 1993

Hull Pottery Newsletter, Dan & Kimberly Pfaff

Konyha, Dee, Personal Correspondence.

Marshall, H.W. Personal interview, July 8, 1983.

Roberts, Brenda. **Ultimate Encyclopedia of Hull Pottery.**

Showers, Gladys. Private correspondence & personal interviews, 1985, 1992, 1993, & 1994

Supnick, Mark. **Collecting Hull Pottery's "Little Red Riding Hood".**

Tomes, Patricia A. National Association of Watch & Clock Collectors. Private correspondence, November 9, 1980.

Whitehouse, Don. Personal interview, 1992.